Wilderness Virginia

Wilderness Virginia

*A Guide to Hiking
Virginia's National
Forest Wilderness
Areas*

By
Steven Carroll
and
Mark Miller

Old Forge Productions

1574 1026
(A7

Library of Congress
Cataloging-in-Publication Data

Carroll, R. Steven. 1969-
Miller, Mark. 1957-
Wilderness Virginia, A Guide to Hiking Virginia's National Forest Wilderness
Areas / by Steven Carroll and Mark Miller
    p. cm.
1. Hiking--Virginia--Guidebooks.
2. Hiking--Guidebooks.

1995   CIP 95-68417
ISBN   0-9646692-1-8

All photos by the authors unless otherwise noted.
Cover photo by Mark Miller
Back cover photo by Steven Carroll

Manufactured in the United States of America

Old Forge Productions, L.L.C.
Route 1, Box 314
Lexington, VA 24450

The authors and Old Forge Productions assume no liability for injury which
may result from activities described in this book.

Furthermore, due to the dynamic nature of the forest, the authors and Old
Forge Productions assume no liability for any inaccuracies of trail descriptions
or distances. All stated times are estimates based on a rate of approximately
2.0 miles per hour. Hiking times will vary based on trail conditions and individual ability.

The authors and Old Forge Productions assume no liability for water quality. All water should be treated before consuming.

To Cindy and Gina
For all your support and encouragement

Acknowledgements

We would like to thank Bill Miller and Michele Elmore for their review of the trail descriptions and their willingness to read through all of them.

USGS for all the fine maps they have created.

USFS representatives for their efforts to preserve these valuable assets and for providing guidance in locating lost roads.

Contents

How To Use This Guide

In order to properly utilize this guide, it is necessary to have an understanding of the layout and information contained within the book. The chapters of this book describe separate wilderness areas. Each chapter provides an introduction, maps, and trail descriptions.

There are two types of maps included in this guide: A road map shows the wilderness in relation to surrounding roads. The locations of parking areas are noted. Topographical maps provide trail locations and a general layout of the land within the wilderness boundaries. Neither road maps nor topographical maps are to scale.

The book contains a wealth of information about each trail. Trail names are followed by a number. This trail number can be found on the topographic map and assists in locating the trail. Trail descriptions are preceeded by a list of general trail information. This information includes length, time, difficulty, elevation change, USGS maps, and trailhead. Times are based on a rate of approximately two mile per hour rate. Trail difficulty is based on three tier scale: easy, moderate, and difficult. The names of the 1:24,000 scale USGS maps are listed as map sources. For other available maps, contact the USGS or the US Forest Service. Having these maps is recommended if off trail hiking is planned.

Following this brief trail information, detailed directions to the trailhead are provided. This is followed by a description of the trail. Information includes: local flora, trail conditions, trail grades, campsites, and possible water sources

This book makes use of several abbreviations. These include:

AT	Appalachian Trail
BRP	Blue Ridge Parkway
CR	County Route
FS	Forest Service
I	Interstate
P	Parking
SR	State Route
USGS	United States Geological Survey

A Brief History of the NWPS

When hiking in a wilderness area it is good to know a little about what wilderness is. An understanding of what went into the creation of the National Wilderness Preservation System (NWPS) should increase a hiker's feeling of responsibility for an area. The history of the NWPS dates back to the beginning of the century and culminates in Virginia in 1984.

The NWPS, signed into law in 1964 by Lyndon Johnson, is the result of much effort to preserve our nations wild lands. The idea that wilderness should be preserved began in the western states in the first part of this century. In 1924 Aldo Leopold, a Forest Service employee, decided to manage 540,000 acres in New Mexico as the Gila Wilderness Reserve. Many wilderness proponents joined together and soon groups such as the Sierra Club and the Wilderness Society were born. These groups were responsible for building support for the wilderness movement. By 1949 a proposal was made to create a national wilderness system. This idea was debated and the final outcome was the passing of the Wilderness Act in 1964.

The Wilderness Act defined "wilderness" and its uses, and also determined areas for inclusion into the system. Wilderness was defined as "...an area where earth and its community are untrammeled by man, where man himself is a visitor who does not remain" (Wilderness Act, 1964). The Act established that wilderness areas would be devoted to the public purposes of recreational, scenic, scientific, educational, conservation, and historical uses (Wilderness Act, 1964). The Act established The NWPS and immediately entered into the system all lands that were previously managed as wilderness. The NWPS also made provisions for adding areas to the system and gave the Forest Service a certain amount of time to complete studies on other areas.

The highly populated East proved problematic for identifying areas to included in the NWPS. The problem in the East was determining what was "untrammeled by man." Virtually every area in the East had been touched by man at one time. After much discussion and legislation, the fate of eastern wilderness ultimately rested with the Forest Service and RARE II. The Forest Service worked for many years preparing its Roadless Area Review and Evaluation (RARE I and RARE II) to evaluate areas best suited for inclusion in the NWPS. Upon the completion of RARE II in 1979, President Carter recommended 15.1 million acres for inclusion in the NWPS. This paved the way for wilderness legislation in each state.

In 1984 the Virginia Wilderness Act designated eleven areas as wilderness. An additional four areas were designated as study areas. These study areas were added to the NWPS in 1987. Today there are more than 80,000 acres of Wilderness land in Virginia. These primitive areas dot the western end of the state. Knowledge of the areas, their locations, purposes, and uses must be expanded or we risk losing them.

Common Sense Hiking

Hiking is a fun, leisure activity. Exploring new trails and new areas of the state are open invitations to excitement and adventure. Common sense suggests that hiking does carry a certain amount of risk. However, this risk can be minimized with good planning and a little forethought. There are several things to consider when planning a hike.

Weather

Weather can be a hiker's best friend or worst enemy. Summer in Virginia brings weather that can best be described as hot and humid. This type of weather can be very dangerous. One reason is dehydration, which results from not drinking enough fluids. While hiking, body temperature rises and fluid is lost as perspiration. The evaporation of perspiration cools the body. If more fluids are lost than are ingested, the result is dehydration. To avoid this condition, drink plenty of fluid before the hike and then remember to drink while on the trail. Look at maps to determine where water might be available, and be sure to purify the water to assure that it is safe to drink. Common sense dictates that a hiker should always carry an adequate supply of water.

Heat exhaustion and heat stroke are potentially life threatening situations and are hazards of hiking in Virginia. Both ailments result when the body is not cooled properly. Heat exhaustion occurs first and, if not treated, can develop into its more fatal cousin - heat stroke. If extensive hiking is planned during warm weather, consult a first-aid guide on the symptoms and treatment of heat exhaustion and heat stroke.

Storms are another aspect of summer weather of which to be aware. Storms, especially in the higher elevations, can develop suddenly and become severe. On Mount Rogers, there is a posted sign warning of the possibility of rapidly changing weather. The sign states that temperatures can drop twenty degrees, and wind speed can increase by twenty miles per hour in less than one hour. If threatening weather presents itself, common sense would dictate finding shelter from the storm. Severe thunderstorms in Virginia can bring with them wind speed of more than fifty miles per hour, driving rain, lightning, and hail. Any one of these conditions could be life threatening.

On bright days, sunburn can be a problem in both summer and

winter. While not immediately life threatening, sunburn can be painful. Sunburn can also significantly increase one's risk of skin cancer. Be aware that on sunny days and even partly sunny days the possibility of sunburn exists. While hiking, remember to wear a hat to protect the face and a shirt to protect the back and arms. Shirts are not completely effective at blocking the sun's rays, especially when wet. Sunblock lotions above SPF 15 are also effective in preventing sunburn.

During the winter months, hikers need to take extra precautions. Two cold weather emergencies to be concerned about are hypothermia and frostbite. Hypothermia results when the body temperature is lowered below the normal temperature. If hypothermia is not treated it can lead to death. Frostbite occurs when skin is exposed to cold and ice crystals form in the body. It usually occurs in the extremities of the body and restricts the blood flow. If hiking when the possibility of cold weather exists, consult a first-aid guide for the symptoms and treatment of frostbite and hypothermia.

Windchill can play a big role in both frostbite and hypothermia. Blowing wind robs the body of heat. Frostbite and hypothermia can occur quickly when the wind is blowing. It is good idea to carry wind proof clothing while hiking, especially if hiking in areas with exposed ridges (ex. Pine Mountain and Mount Rogers).

Plants

Several potentially harmful plants are found in Virginia. Learning to identify harmful plants is the most effective way to avoid them. Poison ivy is the most common problem plant encountered while hiking. Poison ivy is a climbing plant found along many trails. It grows best in sunny open areas like old clearings and trails. This plant has compound leaves of three leaflets. When touched, the plant leaves a residue that causes a skin rash. The rash is characterized by itchy redness and blistering. Treatment usually involves placing lotions on the affected area to keep them dry and reduce the sensation of itching. In severe cases a doctor may need to be consulted. Remember, the best way to avoid the plant is to know what it looks like. After becoming familiar with poison ivy, just stay away from it.

Another group of pontentailly dangerous plants in Virginia are the mushrooms. There are some species which are edible. However, most are not and if you are not familiar with identifying mushrooms, do not eat them. Poisonous mushrooms will usually make one sick, but can be deadly. The best way to deal with mushrooms is leave them alone. It is better to err on the side of caution. Therefore, if not absolutely sure of the variety, do not eat mushrooms.

Stinging nettle is another type of plant that can cause problems while hiking. This plant stands about 24 inches high, with toothed leaves that grow in pairs opposite each other on the stem. The leaves have bristle that contain a watery juice that can produce an intense, but short term itch. The best way to avoid problems with nettles is to wear long pants while hiking.

There are many other plants in Virginia wilderness that may cause allergic or toxic reactions. The best way to avoid them is to get a field guide and educate oneself on their characteristics. Knowing the local flora is a pleasant way to enjoy the outdoors and the best way to keep safe.

Rhododendron in the Spring.

Animals

While hiking, it is important to remember that we are visitors to the forest. The forest is the home of many animals. Although most animals in the forest are small, even the smallest animal when threatened will defend itself. The best way to avoid unwanted problems with animals is to leave them alone. Generally, when left alone, an animal will not feel threatened and therefore will not attempt to defend itself. The rule of thumb is simple - leave the animals alone.

Animals like food and spend most of their time acquiring it. Over the years many animals have learned that hikers represent a supply of food. To avoid problems with animals while on an overnight trip, place a rope over a high limb and suspend the pack above the ground. By placing the pack in the air, animals will be unable to reach it and therefore not eat the food or destroy the pack. The mental image of a bear clawing through a tent wall to get to a pack should be enough to convince anyone to hang their pack.

There are two types of snakes which can be dangerous in the mountains of Virginia. These are rattlesnakes and copperheads. Both snakes will bite when threatened, and both snakes are poisonous. The best defenses against snake bite are good boots for hiking and long pants. Although there are no guarantees that a bite will not occur, they do reduce the odds. The other defense against a snake bite is to know what the snakes look like and where they are most likely to live. Then, when walking in their habitat, be on the lookout. Remember, if bitten by a snake, stay calm and seek medical help quickly. If hiking solo, it is advisable to carry a snake bite kit just to be on the safe side. Having a first-aid guide and knowing the procedure for dealing with snakebites is a must.

Insects are another type of animal in the forest, the most notorious of which is the mosquito. In wet areas, these insects thrive and can make life miserable. When bitten by a mosquito, the area will swell slightly and itch. Try not to scratch the affected area. The best way to avoid bug bites is to wear extra layers of light clothing. One can always buy one of several brands of insect repellent, too. Ticks can also be a problem. The best remedy for ticks is to look for them periodically. If bitten, the best way to remove a tick is with tweezers, taking care to pinch the head and not the body. Follow accepted first-aid procedures and the risk of getting disease from a tick will be lessened.

Rattlesnakes will bite if threatened.

Protecting Yourself

This is a broad category and yet a very important one. There are many general precautions to take which will make a wilderness adventure safer and more enjoyable. When hiking, let someone know were you will be hiking and when you expect to return. Also, know your route of travel including length and level of difficulty. Then assess your ability relative to trail difficulty. Remember, you know your ability best; listen to what your body is telling you. It is better to be safe than sorry.

Always carry a map and a compass. Before entering the wilderness, learn methods of outdoor orienteering. Then if you become lost, you have the skills necessary to find your way out of the woods and back to your vehicle.

Clothing is another important consideration. Good boots are essential. Boots protect against turned ankles, wet feet, and a host of other minor problems that can make a hike miserable. As good as boots are, they are only as good as the socks worn inside them. Wool socks are good for hiking because they stay warm even when wet. There are summer and winter versions of socks that suit various thermal needs. A hat is important, also. A hat protects the head and face from sunburn, keeps the head dry when raining, and prevents blowing winds from cooling the body. A lightweight windbreaker should be carried in case of severe wind, and if waterproof, it can double for protection against the rain.

Finally, the woods around Virginia are open to hunting in the fall and winter. Since the timing of hunting seasons vary from county to county, it is necessary to obtain a schedule from the Fish and Game Commission and plan a hike accordingly. It is best to stay out of the woods during the general firearms season. If planning to hike during hunting season, remember to wear blaze orange and bypass bushwhacks if possible. Blaze orange may not look great but it will reduce the chance of a hunting accident. Deer and turkey seasons are probably the most dangerous, but be aware of any type of hunting activity. We recommend wearing blaze orange during any hunting season. This will significantly reduce the chance of injury.

This list of common sense suggestions is not all inclusive, but it does cover the broad issues. The thing to remember is that if common sense and pre-planning are used most problems will be just minor inconveniences.

Wilderness Ethics

Hiking and camping are wonderful outdoor activities. However, when enjoying the wilderness areas of Virginia several considerations should be made. These considerations are based on the purpose of the National Wilderness Preservation System. When land is included in the NWPS, it enjoys the securities of increased regulation regarding land use. As an individual user of wilderness resources, the outdoor enthusiast should strive to preserve and protect the pristine nature of the wilderness areas. The following guidelines ensures that others can also enjoy the wilderness experience.

Low impact hiking and camping is preferable. When hiking, try to keep group numbers low. A two person group is ideal. Large groups can trample an area quickly, especially when camp is set up. Camp in previously used areas if possible. This reduces the number of areas scarred by man's presence. Pack in a stove and do NOT make a campfire. Leaving dead timber to rot allows natural nutrient cycles to continue and decreases the chance of forest fires.

The pristine beauty of a wilderness is affected by the amount of use it receives. To protect this beauty, care should be taken to prevent overuse. After hiking a trail, remember there are other trails to explore. By experiencing all trails, damage to popular areas is decreased. Possibly the most rewarding aspect of wilderness is the prospect of hiking all day without seeing another person. Temporally spreading out one's use of any particular area increases the chance that others can also enjoy these solitary rewards.

There are some that think these guidelines are too strict. Remember, the areas in question are wilderness areas dedicated to preserving lands where man's influence is greatly unseen. These guidelines are meant to keep the wilderness user's influence, as well as the user himself, greatly unseen. The Forest Service manages large amounts of land in Virginia, and the "multiple use" doctrine insures that there is land somewhere for virtually every forest activity. If an individual's use is not compliant with the wilderness ethic, there is sure to be an area nearby where the activity is allowed. Wilderness preservation is one use of forested lands. Please enjoy wilderness in such a way that will not lessen someone else's experience.

Barbours Creek Wilderness

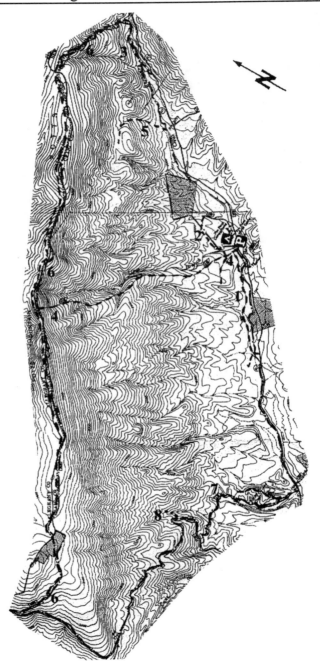

Barbours Creek

The Barbours Creek Wilderness is a 5,700 acre area located in the northwest corner of Craig County, in the New Castle District of the Jefferson National Forest. The wilderness is located approximately thirty miles northwest of Roanoke, Virginia. Barbours Creek was declared a wilderness area in 1987.

The wilderness is located on the eastern side of Potts Mountain with the crest of Potts Mountain forming the western boundary of the roadless area. Barbours Creek and County Route 617 form the eastern boundary, while Forest Service road 176 forms the southern boundary. In and around the wilderness area, there are approximately twenty miles of trail. The Lipes Branch Trail is the only maintained trail within this primitive area. All other trails are old roads in various states of decay. Water is scarce along the crest of Potts Mountain and should be carried. However, water is available in most other regions of the wilderness. The area sees little usage except during hunting season and, therefore, provides solitude for the avid backwoods hiker.

The forest of Barbours Creek is comprised of two major types. The first is the oak-hickory forest which is found along the drier slopes of the Allegheny Mountains. The second forest type is found along Barbours Creek and in some mountain hollows. Very large white pine, hemlock and white oak can be seen. Rhododendron is found in abundance in these areas, too.

There are several interesting areas in the Barbours Creek Wilderness. The first is a large bald area located just outside the western boundary on the top of Potts Mountain. This bald is approximately fifty acres in size, and affords a spectacular view. To reach the bald, see the Potts Mountain Trail description. The other area of interest is on Forest Service road 176. This area is an easy to reach rock formation. The rocks are spread pell-mell throughout a small creek bed and can provide some fun scrambling.

One note of caution: This area is a favorite for hunters and many signs of hunting activity are visible while hiking. There are many deer stands located near the bald on the top of Potts Mountain. Additionally, many hunting camps are located along County Route 617.

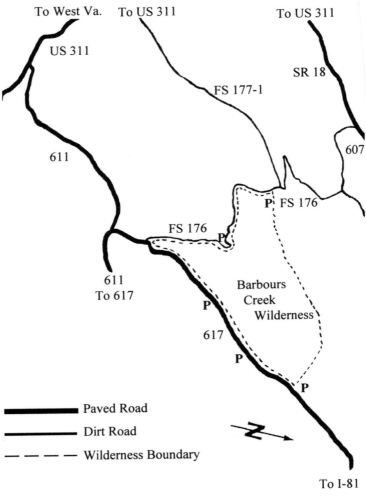

To West Va. To US 311 To US 311

US 311

SR 18

FS 177-1

611

607

FS 176

P FS 176

FS 176 P

611
To 617

P

Barbours
Creek
Wilderness

617

P

P

━━━━ Paved Road

──── Dirt Road

— — — Wilderness Boundary

To I-81

Note: US 311 South leads to Roanoke, and SR 18 leads to
Covington.

14

Barbours Creek Trail 1

Length: 1.3 Miles (One Way)
Time: 45 minutes
Elevation Change: 100 Feet
Difficulty: Easy
USGS Map: New Castle
Trailhead: Lipes Branch Trailhead on CR 617

How To Get There

Take I-64 West toward Covington, Virginia. Take Exit #21 and turn left at the stop sign on CR 696. Travel 0.2 of a mile and turn right on CR 616. After 5.5 miles, there is a "T" intersection. Turn right and continue 6.8 miles on CR 616. Travel 4.6 miles and take a left on CR 617. Proceed 7.2 miles to the Lipes Branch Trailhead parking area located on the right just past The Pines Campground.

From Roanoke, take I-81 to Exit #140 and take US 311 North. Travel 1.3 miles and take a left at the stop light. Proceed 24 miles and turn right on CR 611. Travel 5 miles and turn left on 617. Proceed 4.8 miles to a parking area on the left.

Trail Description

This trail is a short, scenic trail along Barbours Creek to the south of the Lipes Branch Trail. This trail, like many of the trails in the Barbours Creek Wilderness Area is actually the remains of an old road. The trail is very easy and winds slowly downhill at a very gradual rate. The trail is in good condition which makes hiking pleasant.

The Barbours Creek Trail begins near the trailhead for the Lipes Branch Trail. To locate the beginning of the trail, hike the Lipes Branch Trail about 50 yards to a clearing. In this clearing the Barbours Creek Trail exits the Lipes Branch Trail to the left. There are no signs but the exit is very clear. The trail passes through the clearing and enters a stand of small hardwoods, many of which are dogwoods.

Quite suddenly, the trail leaves these small trees behind and enters a stand of huge white pine and cove hardwoods such as tulip poplar, red oak, and white oak. The trail is flat and easy. There is another clearing on the left as the trail bends to the left. This clearing is encircled by huge white pines. The clearing is about 0.25 miles

15

from the trailhead. The trail bends right and continues its easy grade.

There is another small clearing on the right with a small road leading into this area. This clearing offers a great place for an overnight stay. The trees are tall and very beautiful. Just beyond this clearing lies another small clearing. The trail crosses a dry branch about 0.75 miles from the trailhead. At approximately 1.0 miles the trail enters another small clearing. At the next clearing, there is a trail to the right. This trail climbs for about 0.5 miles to a small clearing. There is a site for camping in this location.

The trail continues its easy grade with no major obstacles. Just before reaching Barbours Creek, there is another short trail to the right. This trail goes to a large clearing with rows of white pine. The most difficult aspect of this trail is the Barbours Creek crossing. The crossing is an old ford, however, the water can be deep. It is best to take off footwear. The other option is to walk downstream approximately 50 yards and cross the creek on an old log. On the other side, there is a wilderness sign. CR 617 is approximately 0.1 miles from the creek crossing.

Campground Trail   2

Length: 0.5 Miles
Time: 30 Minutes
Elevation Change: 50 Feet
Difficulty: Easy
USGS Map: New Castle
Trailhead: The Pines Campground

<u>How To Get There</u>

Take I-64 West toward Covington, Virginia. Take Exit #21 and turn left at the stop sign on CR 696. Travel 0.2 of a mile and turn right on CR 616. After 5.5 miles, there is a "T" intersection. Turn right and continue 6.8 miles on CR 616. Travel 4.6 miles and take a left on CR 617. Proceed 6.2 miles to The Pines Campground. The trail is located near the back of the campground.

From Roanoke, take I-81 to Exit #140 and take US 311 North. Travel 1.3 miles and take a left at the stop light. Proceed 24 miles and turn right on CR 611. Travel 5 miles and turn left on CR 617. Proceed 5.1 miles to The Pines Campground. The trail is located near the back of the campground.

Trail Description

This is a short trail which connects the camping area with the wilderness area. The trail is located at the end of the campground loop. The trail is very easy and short. The trail is well maintained and is marked with yellow blazes.

The trail enters the woods from the campground. The forest is predominantly an oak-hickory forest with many trees reaching large sizes. The trail circles around a large hill located near the campground. Shortly after entering the woods, there is a small wilderness sign. Just beyond this sign, the trail crosses a small creek on an old wooden bridge.

After a short climb, there is a switchback to the left, followed by a gradual descent to a small creek. The trail parallels this creek until connecting with Lipes Branch. Here it crosses the creek near a horse trail sign. After crossing the creek, there is a short climb followed by a flat section. It is in this flat region that the Campground Trail joins the Lipes Branch Trail.

A road across Potts Mountain.

Creek Trail   3

Length: 1.1 Miles (One Way)
Time: 1 Hour
Elevation Change: 150 Feet
Difficulty: Easy
USGS Map: Jordan Mines
Trailhead: Potts Mountain Jeep Road on CR 617

How To Get There

Take I-64 West toward Covington, Virginia. Take Exit #21 and turn left at the stop sign on CR 696. Travel 0.2 miles and turn right on CR 616. After 5.5 miles, there is a "T" intersection. Turn right and continue 6.8 miles on CR 616. Travel 4.6 miles and take a left on CR 617. Proceed 4.3 miles and turn right on the Potts Mountain Jeep Trail. There is a small ford of Barbours Creek, but it is not too difficult. Park at the point where the jeep trail turns right and heads up the mountain.

From Roanoke, take I-81 to Exit #140 and take US 311 North. Travel 1.3 miles and take a left at the stop light. Proceed 24 miles and turn right on CR 611. Travel 5 miles and turn left on CR 617. Proceed 7.7 miles to the Potts Mountain Jeep Trail and turn left. There is a small ford of Barbours Creek, but it is not too difficult. Park at the point where the jeep trail turns right and heads up the mountain.

Trail Description

This trail is a very short "out and back;" however, by hiking along the road, the route can be made into a loop. An old road grade lays the foundation for the trail which parallels Barbours Creek. The trail passes though stands of poplar, red and sugar maple, hickory, and oak. There are also thickets of rhododendron and mountain laurel. The trail is relatively easy with the only difficult sections being one ford of the creek and a short climb to the road near the end of the trail.

The trail begins by crossing a rock barrier followed by a slow descent to Barbours Creek. The creek is on the left. After about 0.5 miles, the trail crosses the creek and climbs steeply to the road. Just before reaching the paved road, there is a dirt road which bears to the right. This road leads back to the creek. After about 0.25 miles, the clear road ends, and the trail becomes slightly overgrown. The path again climbs back to the main road. Just prior to reaching the main road, there is an old Forest Service sign and another old road which travels downhill. This road leads toward the creek, but stops upon reaching a small clearing.

Lipes Branch Trail   4

Length: 2.0 Miles (One Way)
Time: 3 Hours
Elevation Change: 1,950 Feet
Difficulty: Moderately Difficult
USGS Map: New Castle
Trailhead: CR 617

How To Get There

Take I-64 West toward Covington, Virginia. Take Exit #21 and turn left at the stop sign on CR 696. Travel 0.2 miles and turn right on CR 616. After 5.5 miles, there is a "T" intersection. Turn right and continue 6.8 miles on CR 616. Travel 4.6 miles and take a left on CR 617. Proceed 7.2 miles. The Lipes Branch Trailhead parking area is located on the right just past The Pines Campground.

From Roanoke, take Exit #140 and take US 311 North. Travel 1.3 miles and take a left at the stop light. Proceed 24 miles and turn right on CR 611. Travel 5 miles and turn left on CR 617. Proceed 4.8 miles to a parking area on the left.

Trail Description

The Lipes Branch Trail is a short two mile trail that climbs from the base of Potts Mountain to its crest. The trail is moderately difficult. The beginning is relatively flat, while the end is fairly steep. The trail begins in a hardwood forest of hickory, oak, and maple. The forest near the end of the trail is comprised of drier species, such as chestnut oak and pine. The path is marked with yellow blazes. There are also orange blazes; however, the yellow blazes mark the trail all the way to the top of Potts Mountain.

The trail begins at a Forest Service information center. The grade at the beginning of the trail is quite easy. There is a small glade shortly up the trail. Just after entering the glade, there is a trail to the left that follows Barbours Creek (See Barbours Creek Trail description). The forest species include cove hardwoods such as red oak, white oak, and tulip poplar. Just past the glade, there is a trail to the left that is marked with orange blazes. This trail follows an old road through a couple of clearings before reaching a dead end. There are several areas adequate for camping. A short distance beyond this trail junction is a second trail on the right which leads to the Lipes Branch Campground. There is a small sign indicating the trail junction (See Campground Trail description). This junction is about 0.25 miles from the trailhead.

At approximately 0.6 miles, the climb becomes more moderate after a left bend and a very short steep climb. After the climb, the trail bends to the right, and the path begins a steady ascent up the shoulder of Potts Mountain. In this region mountain laurel, pine, and chestnut oak are common.

The trail makes a short dip and crosses a small dry branch. On the other side of the branch, the trail becomes slightly more steep and more difficult. The trail bends to the right and begins to contour along the side of the mountain followed by another bend to the right and more steady climbing. At 1.4 miles, the trail has a switchback to the left and another to the right before the final assent to the top of the mountain. Just before the top is reached, there is windfall, but fortunately not across the trail. At the top, the trail "T's" into the Potts Mountain Jeep Trail (See Potts Mountain Trail description), and a small sign marks the the Lipes Branch Trail. There is also a small clearing at the top of the mountain. The junction with the Jeep Trail is 2.0 miles from the trailhead.

Pond Trail   5

Length: 1.1 Miles (One Way)
Time: 45 Minutes
Elevation Change: 500 Feet
Difficulty: Easy
USGS Maps: New Castle, Jordan Mines
Trailhead: CR 617

How To Get There

Take I-64 West toward Covington, Virginia. Take Exit #21 and turn left at the stop sign. Travel 0.2 miles and turn right on CR 616. After 5.5 miles, there is a "T" intersection. Turn right and continue 6.8 miles on CR 616. Take a left on CR 617 and travel 5.9 miles to a small road on the right. Watch closely for this road. Take a right and park in the small clearing.

From Roanoke, take I-81 to Exit #140 and take US 311 North. Travel 1.3 miles and take a left at the stop light. Proceed 24 miles and turn right on CR 611. Travel 5 miles and turn left on CR 617. Proceed 6.1 miles to a small road on the left. Watch closely for the road. Park in the small clearing.

<u>Trail Description</u>

This trail follows an old road along the west side of Barbours Creek and then turns up a hollow. After clearing the hollow, the trail turns more southerly and terminates near a clearing and an old pond. This trail is short and steep. For one seeking an out of the way place to camp, this trail fits the bill.

The trail begins at a small clearing on the east side of the creek. There is a small wilderness sign at the creek bank. The first task is crossing the creek. This is not difficult when the water is low; however, if the water is up it may be advisable to take off footwear. On the other side of the creek, the trail turns in a northerly direction and follows the Barbours Creek for a short distance. This part of the trail is quite easy.

Near a dry creek bed, about 0.25 miles from the trailhead, the trail turns left and quickly climbs up the mountain. The trail enters a narrow ravine and crosses the dry creek several times. After the fourth crossing, the trail's grade becomes easy. The forest is composed primarily of hardwoods such as oak, maple, and hickory.

At 0.8 miles, the trail enters a clearing and then exits on the far side through a small pine grove. Just beyond the pines, there is a small man-made pond. Past the pond, the trail crosses another dry creek and starts a short uphill climb. The trail ends just past the dry creek about 1.1 miles from the beginning.

Potts Mountain Trail   6

Length: 7.3 Miles (One Way)
Time: 4 Hours
Elevation Change: 1,650 Feet
Difficulty: Moderately Difficult
USGS Map: Jordan Mines, New Castle and Potts Creek
Trailhead: FS 176 and CR 617

A pink lady's slipper

<u>How To Get There</u>

Take I-64 West toward Covington, Virginia. Take Exit #21 and turn left at the stop sign on CR 696. Travel 0.2 miles and turn right on CR 616. After 5.5 miles, there is a "T" intersection. Turn right and continue 6.8 miles on CR 616. Travel 4.6 miles and take a left on CR 617. Proceed 4.5 miles and turn right on the Potts Mountain Jeep Trail. The jeep trail has a small ford but the ford is not too difficult. The jeep trail makes a right and continues up the mountain. Park here if you do not have a 4-wheel drive vehicle. To reach the upper parking area, continue 5.4 miles on CR 617 and turn right on FS 176. Near the crest of the mountain, there is a parking area on the right.

From Roanoke, take I-81 to Exit #140 and take US 311 North. Travel 1.3 miles and take a left at the stop light. Proceed 24 miles and turn right on CR 611. Travel 5 miles and turn left on CR 617. Travel 2.3 miles to FS 176 and turn left. Near the crest of the mountain is a parking area on the right. The lower parking area is located 5.4 miles farther up CR 617. Turn left on the Potts Mountain Jeep Road and proceed about 0.25 miles to a parking area.

<u>Trail Description</u>

At the parking area, there are two distinct trails, the first leads down along the creek (See Creek Trail description) while the second is the jeep road up the mountain. This road climbs rapidly to the top of Potts Mountain. Once on the ridge top, the trail follows the crest to FS 176. The Potts Mountain Jeep Trail is not in the wilderness itself, but forms the northern and western boundaries of the Barbours Creek Wilderness Area.

The trail is initially very steep. There are six switchbacks as the road climbs to the ridge top. This section is very steep and can be extremely muddy in wet weather. At approximately 0.6 miles the switchbacks end and the grade becomes moderate. The forest type throughout this area is dry slope species such as chestnut oak and pine.

After about 1.0 miles, there is a FS gate. Just past this gate and to the left is a dirt barrier and a road to the right. This road leads to a small clearing where it ends. Once past the gate, the grade becomes easy. At 1.25 miles the jeep trail intersects with several other jeep trails in a gap near the ridge top. Bear left at these intersections to continue along the ridge.

The trail begins to climb, and the grade becomes moderate. Near the top of this short climb, on the right, there is an old stone fence still in very good condition. Just past this rock wall the ridge flattens out. There is a significant amount of wind damage in this area dominated by red oak, hickory, and large chestnut oak. There are also many blackberry and wineberry bushes, as well as a small clearing populated by old apple trees. The clearing, at an elevation of 3,435 feet, is located about 2.3 miles from the trailhead.

From this clearing, the trail travels downhill to another small clearing. At approximately 3.2 miles is a small gap and an orange blazed trail exits to the left. However, this trail ends after a short distance. The main trail becomes very steep and climbs up to a rocky ridge top. There are beautiful views to the east along the rocky ridge. A jeep road intersects from the right, and the jeep trail becomes more rutted from heavy use. Also, there are many deer stands nearby so be careful during hunting season.

About 0.3 miles from the gap, the trail enters a large bald area that is suitable for camping. There are good views of Bald Mountain to the east and the spire of Nicholls Knob to the north. Next, the trail enters another wooded area containing beautiful, gnarled chestnut oaks. At the next small clearing, the Lipes Branch Trail intersects with the Potts Mountain Jeep Trail from the left (See Lipes Branch Trail description). This trail junction is approximately 3.9 miles from the trailhead.

From the junction with the Lipes Branch Trail, the Potts Mountain Jeep Trail takes on the appearance of a rugged dirt road. At the junction the trail crosses a small meadow. After reentering the trees there are some rocks to the right that afford views of the Potts Creek area of Alleghany County, Virginia. The walk continues along the top of the mountain at an elevation of nearly 3,800 feet. The trail makes an "S" turn around a wet section at approximately 6.2 miles and continues across the ridgetop. The road passes several turnouts where hunters often camp. When the trail begins to turn and descend, the intersection with FS 176 is near. FS 176 is reached at 7.3 miles.

Two Interesting Areas   7, 8

<u>How to Get There</u>

Take I-64 West toward Covington, Virginia. Take Exit #21 and turn left at the stop sign on CR 696. Travel 0.2 of a mile and turn right on CR 616. After 5.5 miles, there is a "T" intersection. Turn right and continue 6.8 miles on CR 616. Travel 4.6 miles and take a left on CR 617. Proceed 9.7 miles and turn right on FS 176. Travel 1.3 miles to a small parking area on the right or continue 2.5 miles to another small parking area on the right.

From Roanoke, take Exit #140 and take US 311 North. Travel

1.3 miles and take a left at the stop light. Proceed 24 miles and turn right on CR 611. Travel 5 miles and turn left on 617. Travel 2.3 miles to FS 176 and follow the directions described above.

Trail Description

The first area is marked with orange blazes. There is a short trail that climbs quickly to a narrow gap. Upon passing through the gap, the land begins to slope down to a large flat area. There is no trail but the area offers adventurous bushwhacking.

The second area is also marked with orange blazes. There is a short ditch to cross and then a small road. About 50 yards from FS 176, there is a trail to the right. The trail has a very steep drop and leads to a large boulder field that is fun to explore.

Beartown
Wilderness

Beartown

The Beartown Wilderness is located approximately twenty miles northwest of Wytheville, Virginia. The wilderness, located in the Wythe Ranger District of the Jefferson National Forest, encompasses an area of approximately 6,375 acres. The primitive area is located in the southeastern corner of Tazewell County. The area was designated as wilderness in 1984.

The Beartown Wilderness is located on the southern rim of Burkes Garden, a natural bowl completely surrounded by Garden Mountain. The crests of Chestnut Ridge and Clinch Mountain form the eastern and western boundary, respectively. Roaring Fork is the major drainage of the Beartown Wilderness and Coon Branch, Bear Camp Creek and Cove Branch are major feeders into the Roaring Fork. Cove Branch has an unusual headwater source: a sphagnum bog located at approximately 4,500 feet. The elevation ranges from a low of approximately 2,400 feet on the Roaring Fork to 4,710 at the top of Garden Mountain. Hutchinson Rock, an expanse of rock cliffs, is located on the long northeastern arm of the wilderness.

The wilderness has only one well-maintained trail within its boundary, and this is the Appalachian Trail. There are many old roads into the wilderness. Many of these roads suffer from windfall and storm damage, but the damage should not hinder hiking. These old roads and the Appalachian trail provide over twenty-two miles of hiking adventure. Water is plentiful throughout most of the wilderness. The only area of limited water availability is the ridge of Clinch Mountain.

The forest in the Beartown Wilderness is very diverse. The high elevations located within the boundaries support a thriving northern red spruce forest. Northern hardwoods can also be found within the wilderness area with yellow birch being one example. Cove hardwoods such as yellow poplar and white oak are common along the Roaring Fork. Large hemlock and white pine are represented in large numbers in these sheltered coves. The eastern slope of Clinch Mountain is more representative of the oak-hickory forests common in most parts of Virginia, while chestnut oak dominates the ridge of Clinch Mountain.

A sphagnum bog located between Garden Mountain and Clinch Mountain is a truly unique ecological feature of the Beartown Wilderness. The bog is almost completely surrounded by huge rhododendron thickets and low impenetrable hardwood thickets. The bog is a beautifully scenic area and is protected by its remoteness.

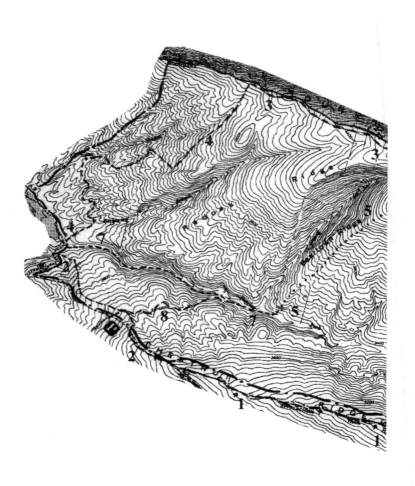

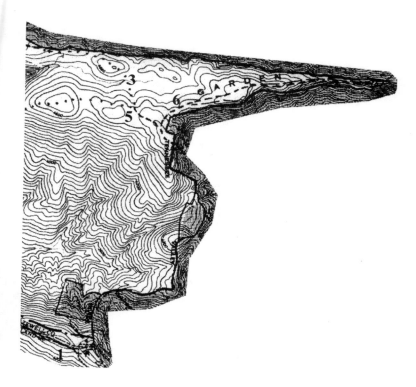

Small pools of water are located throughout the bog, and the Cove Branch lazily meanders through these ponds before its crashing rush to Roaring Fork.

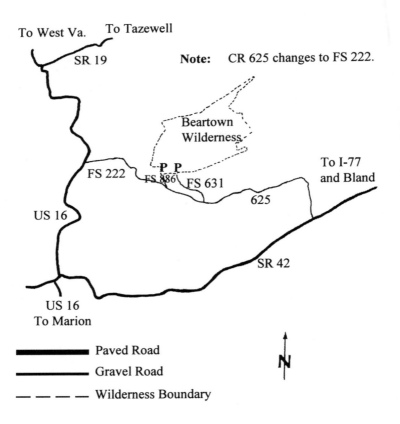

Appalachian Trail 1

Length: 2.5 Miles (One Way)
Time: 2 Hours
Elevation Change: 700 Feet
Difficulty: Easy
USGS Map: Hutchinson Rock
Trailhead: FS Road 631

How to Get There

Take I-81 to I-77 North at Wytheville take Exit #72. Travel north on I-77 to Exit #52. At the stop sign turn left onto US 52-42. Travel 4.2 miles and turn right on SR 42. Proceed 10.2 miles and turn right on CR 625. At 0.4 miles, there is a "Y" in the road, bear to the right. Travel 7.6 miles to FS 631 and turn right. Travel 2.6 miles up the mountain to an earth barriers. This is the parking area. One note of caution, FS 631 is a rough road and requires a vehicle with a high wheel base.

Trail Description

As the Appalachian Trail reaches the crest of Chestnut Ridge, the Chestnut Ridge Trail joins the AT from the left (See Chestnut Ridge Trail description). The AT turns right at the ridge and continues climbing at a steady pace. The trail enters an upland meadow with panoramic views in all directions. There is a pond on the left about 0.5 miles after entering the meadow.

The AT crosses an old fence line and then enters the woods again. There is a brief descent shortly after entering the woods. About 2.3 miles from the trail junction, an old road crosses the AT and goes downhill on both the right and left sides of the trail. There is another small pond on the left just past this road.

The trail begins to climb again and enters another small clearing. This clearing is the summit of Chestnut Ridge and has an elevation of 4,408 feet. There is an AT shelter at the top called the Chestnut Knob Shelter. A Beartown Wilderness sign is visible here, but there are no trails from this point into the wilderness. There is a spectacular view into Burkes Garden. Burkes Garden is natural bowl surrounded on all sides by Garden Mountain.

Chestnut Ridge Trail   2

Length: 1.8 Miles (One Way)
Time: 2 Hours
Elevation Change: 1,300 Feet
Difficulty: Moderate
USGS Map: Hutchinson Rock
Trailhead: See "How to Get There" below

How to Get There

Take I-81 to I-77 North at Wytheville take Exit #72. Travel north on I-77 to Exit #52. At the stop sign turn left onto US 52-42. Travel 4.2 miles and turn right on SR 42. Proceed 10.2 miles and turn right on CR 625. At 0.4 miles there is a "Y" in the road. Bear to the right. Travel 7.6 miles to FS 631. Continue straight for another 1.9 miles to a small road on the right. Watch carefully for this road as it is unmarked and easy to miss. Take this right and travel 1.3 miles to the ford at Roaring Fork. Park at the ford. This is a rough road and requires a vehicle with a high wheel base.

Trail Description

This trail climbs quickly from the trailhead near the Roaring Fork to the Roaring Fork Connector Trail before connecting with the AT near the top of Chestnut Ridge. There is a great deal of downfall from the trailhead to the Roaring Fork Connector Trail which makes hiking difficult. The trail passes through a forest of mixed hardwoods.

The trailhead is located about 0.1 miles up the road from the parking area near the Roaring Fork ford. The trail is slightly overgrown with grass and trees, but it is easy to follow. The path is steep and quickly leaves the sounds of the Roaring Fork behind. There are many trees across the trail, however, this windfall does not create many difficulties.

At 0.9 miles, the trail crosses the Roaring Fork Connector Trail (See Roaring Fork Connector Trail description) and continues to climb. There is still a great deal of storm damage. Then, quite suddenly, the trees give way to a high upland meadow. Shortly after entering the meadow lies the junction with the AT (See AT description). This is 1.8 miles from the trailhead.

Clinch Mountain Trail 3

Length: 2.7 Miles (One Way)
Time: 3.0 Hours
Elevation Change: 600 Feet
Difficulty: Moderate
USGS Map: Hutchinson Rock
Trailhead: Junction with Coon Branch Trail

How to Get There

Via the Coon Branch Trail.

Trail Description

The Clinch Mountain Trail is reached via the Coon Branch Trail (See Coon Branch Trail description). The Clinch Mountain Trail is an old road which travels along the ridge of Clinch Mountain. This trail description begins at the junction of the Coon Branch Trail and describes the Clinch Mountain Trail as it moves in a northeasterly direction toward the summit of Garden Mountain. The forest type located throughout this region is upland hardwoods with chestnut oak being the dominant species. As Clinch Mountain joins Garden Mountain farther north, hemlock, white pine, and red spruce become the dominant species.

The trail follows the crest of Clinch Mountain. About 0.5 miles from the start of the trail a road leads downhill to the right. This road is a dead end. Just beyond this intersection is another road that bears to the left. Go right following the road less traveled. This trail is at times grassy and is always covered by leaves. The trail climbs gradually to a dead end and an old turn-around. The turn-around is 1.5 miles from the junction with the Coon Branch Trail. There is a small clearing located in this area. The trail stops here.

The daring, however, can continue along the ridge. There is a large rhododendron thicket to contend with about 0.5 miles from the clearing. There is a trail cut through the thicket. Just be patient and look for the opening. Once on the other side of the thicket there are views to the west. Angling slightly downward toward the Cove Branch can be a rewarding experience. There is a sphagnum bog located at the headwaters of the Cove Branch. The foliage and wildlife diversity of this area is wonderful. The bog is located about 0.8 miles from the clearing and the old turn-around.

After crossing the bog and the Cove Branch, there is another Rhododendron thicket after 0.4 miles. Climb the trail toward the east ridge and look for the opening in the thicket. This is the access to the top of Garden Mountain (See Garden Mountain Bushwhack description).

Coon Branch   4

Length: 3.0 Miles (One Way)
Time: 3.0 Hours
Elevation Change: 1,600 Feet
Difficulty: Difficult
USGS Map: Hutchinson Rock
Trailhead: See "How to Get There" below

How to Get There

Take I-81 to I-77 North, at Wytheville take Exit #72. Travel north on I-77 to Exit #52. At the stop sign, turn left onto US 52-42. Travel 4.2 miles and turn right on SR 42. Proceed 10.2 miles and turn right on CR 625. At 0.4 miles there is a "Y" in the road. Bear to the right. Travel 7.6 miles to FS 631. Continue straight for another 1.9 miles to a small road on the right. Watch carefully for this road as it is unmarked and easy to miss. Travel 1.3 miles to the ford at Roaring Fork. This is a rough road and requires a vehicle with a high wheel base.

Trail Description

The Coon Branch Trail climbs from the Roaring Fork parking area to the ridge top of Clinch Mountain. The trail follows an old road grade and is generally steep and rocky. There is a fair amount of downfall across the trail, but the downfall is usually easy to avoid. The trail begins by passes through a mixed hardwood forest of hickory, oak, and maple, and then acsends into a forest which is dotted with red spruce and hemlock.

From the parking area, the first obstacle to overcome is the Roaring Fork. The water is usually knee deep where the Coon Branch Trail crosses the Roaring Fork. Once on the other side, the trail will begin to climb. The ascent begins gradually but soon becomes difficult. There will be a series of switchbacks as the trail climbs to the ridge. The trail parallels the Roaring Fork briefly but turns away

Rich Mountain as seen from Garden Mountain.

from the fork and heads to the Bearcamp Branch. After about 0.25 miles, the trail crosses the Bearcamp Branch. At the crossing, there are remains of an old bridge. Just past the crossing is a sign for the Beartown Wilderness Area. The trail bends to the left and becomes steeper. After the switchback to the right, the grade is moderate but there are still several more switchbacks.

At 0.6 miles, the trail reaches Coon Branch and parallels the creek for some distance. Although the trail actually never crosses the branch, the creek can be heard tumbling down the mountain to the right. At this point, there is some downfall across the trail. The downfall is not extensive and is easily bypassed. The trail is gullied and washed out in many places and footing can be treacherous.

The trail becomes almost level near an old hunting campsite about 2.0 miles from Roaring Fork. However, the respite is brief. After the campsite, the trail turns to the right and begins a very steep climb to the shoulder of Clinch Mountain. This climb lasts approximately 0.3 miles. On the shoulder, the trail makes a bend to the left and the grade becomes more moderate.

Finally, at 3.0 miles the trail reaches the crest of Clinch Mountain (See Clinch Mountain Trail description). There is an old road along the ridge top. A left on the road leads out of the wilderness and to US 16. A right on the ridge follows the road farther into the heart of the Beartown Wilderness.

Garden Mountain Bushwhack   5

Length: 2.6 Miles (One Way)
Time: 3 Hours
Elevation Change: 1,700 Feet
Difficulty: Very Difficult
USGS Map: Hutchinson Rock
Trailhead: End Of Roaring Fork Connector Trail

How to Get There

Via the Roaring Fork Connector Trail.

Trail Description

To reach the summit of Garden Mountain is not an easy task. First, hike down to the Roaring Fork (See Roaring Fork Connector Trail description). Once at the creek, hike up the creek. When the road ends, just past the Cove Branch, cross Roaring Fork and begin to climb. There is no trail, but the way is clear. Just climb uphill. This is a very steep mountain to climb so take it slow and easy.

After about 1.4 miles, near the lower crest, the mountain begins to flatten out The first plateau is not the true peak. Once on the ridge crest, hike in a northeasterly direction. There will be a small loss in elevation as the crest has a small saddle. Once the saddle is crossed, tremendous rhododendron thickets are visible. These thickets must be crossed in order to reach the top of the mountain. Do not despair, as there is a trail through the rhododendron, but one has to look carefully for the opening. As elevation is gained, stay close to the thicket and be on the lookout for two landmarks. The first is survey tape which is replaced regularly. The second is a small fire pit and a campsite near the opening. This opening is 0.8 miles from the first crest.

Once on the trail, you may feel like Moses as he parted the Red Sea. The trail comes out of the thicket near the top of Garden Mountain. This short section of trail is about 0.2 miles. When the trail clears the thicket, there is a trail junction. The left path leads to Hutchinson Rock (See Hutchinson Rock Trail description), and the right leads to the top of Garden Mountain. Follow the path 0.2 miles, up to the clearing at the top. The clearing is surrounded by red spruce. There are beautiful views to the south and east. This clearing is a great place to camp and there is water nearby. A stone fire pit has also been constructed. However, the pit is located in a dry grassy area and fire could be dangerous.

A window-in-the-rocks on Garden Mountain.

Hutchinson Rock Trail   6

Length: 1.9 Miles (One Way)
Time: 1.25 Hours
Elevation Change: 250 Feet
Difficulty: Easy
USGS Map: Hutchinson Rock
Trailhead: On the Top of Garden Mountain

How to Get There

Via the Clinch Mountain Trail/Bushwhack or the Garden Mountain Bushwhack.

Trail Description

The trail to Hutchinson Rock winds across the western end of Garden Mountain and the northern end of the Beartown Wilderness. The trail has two distinct flavors. The first part of the trail winds through an area of marsh covered by thick, low brush. Without a trail, exploring this area would be impossible. The second part of the trail travels through a forest of mixed hardwoods and evergreens.

The trail begins after clearing the rhododendron thicket described in the Garden Mountain Bushwhack. Instead of turning right and hiking to the summit of Garden Mountain, the Hutchinson Rock Trail turns left and leads downhill. Again, stay close to the thicket as there is another opening through the rhododendron.

Once into the thicket, the trail is very obvious. There is only one way to go and to leave the trail would be difficult. The trail continues down for some distance before climbing again toward Hutchinson Rock. The trail is completely surrounded by low brush, and the brush is just high enough to block any views of the surrounding countryside. About 0.4 miles into the brush is a large rock. The view from this rock is quite impressive. To the north and east is Burkes Garden, while to the west is a nice view of the cliff covered ridge of Rich Mountain.

At 1.2 miles, the trail descends through a rocky area and the whole complexion of the trail changes. As the brush is left behind the forest reestablishes itself. The trees are predominantly yellow birch and red spruce with some hemlock and other mixed hardwoods. The trail becomes less obvious, but the trees have been blazed with an axe and the trail markings are very evident.

The ridge narrows and the trail meanders along the side of the ridge. While on this section, about 1.5 miles from the trailhead, look out for the window-in-the-rock (See picture, p. 43). Once past this rock, the trail climbs to the ridge top. The trail ends at a 4-wheeler trail. This junction is at 1.7 miles. However, do not stop here. The best views in the wilderness are just a short 0.2 miles ahead. Continue to follow the ridge top to Hutchinson Rock. Hutchinson Rock can be climbed with little difficulty. The best way to climb is from the west side. The view from the rock is spectacular and makes the hike worthwhile.

Roaring Fork Trail   7

Length: 1.7 Miles (One Way)
Time: 1 Hour
Elevation Change: 550 Feet
Difficulty: Easy
USGS Map: Hutchinson Rock
Trailhead: FS 631

How to Get There

Take I-81 to I-77 North at Wytheville take Exit #72. Travel north on I-77 to Exit #52. At the stop sign turn left onto US 52-42. Travel 4.2 miles and turn right on SR 42. Proceed 10.2 miles and turn right on CR 625. At 0.4 miles there is a "Y" in the road, bear to the right. Travel 7.6 miles to FS 631. Continue straight another 1.9 miles to a small road on the right. Watch carefully for this road as it is unmarked and easy to miss. Travel 1.3 miles to the ford at the Roaring Fork. This is a rough road and requires a vehicle with a high wheel base.

Trail Description

The Roaring Fork Trail follows the Roaring Fork. The Roaring Fork is the major drainage for the Beartown Wilderness Area. This trail is actually an old road which parallels the native trout waters of the Fork. The creek, with head waters located high on Garden Mountain, flows quietly down the hollow. The water is clear and undisturbed. The trail travels through beautiful stands of mixed cove hardwoods like poplar, yellow birch, oak, and hickory. There is also occasional Frazier magnolia.

Garden Mountain

The Roaring Fork Trail begins at the trailhead located at a parking area just before the Roaring Fork ford. There is a large boulder barrier located at the trailhead. The trail has an easy grade initially. The trail passes through a small grassy area and then enters a wooded area. Once into the woods, about 0.4 miles, the trail crosses the creek. Just beyond the creek crossing are some very large and imposing cliffs to the right.

At 0.6 miles, the trail crosses the creek and there is a small amount of windfall. These downed trees are probably the most difficult aspect of the trail. Once past this first downfall, the trail crosses the creek again. This crossing is 1.0 miles from the trailhead. The creek crossings are not difficult unless the water is high. There is more windfall, but again it is not too difficult. There are some delightful water slides and waterfalls throughout this section of the trail. However, none of the falls are very large. The trail grade continues to be very gradual.

At 1.3 miles, the creek is crossed again. Once on the other side, the trail climbs to the junction of the Roaring Fork Connector Trail (See Roaring Fork Connector Trail description). There is a very nice open campsite located where the two trails connect. Taking a right at the junction leads up Chestnut Ridge . Going straight leads to a dead end, but there is a small waterfall where Cove Branch drains into Roaring Fork. Just past this creek junction is the best access to the top of Garden Mountain (See Garden Mountain Trail description).

Roaring Fork Connector Trail   8

Length: 1.7 Miles (One Way)
Time: 1 Hour
Elevation Change: 150 Feet
Difficulty: Easy
USGS Map: Hutchinson Rock
Trailhead: FS Road 631

How to Get There

Take I-81 to I-77 North at Wytheville take Exit #72. Travel north on I-77 to Exit #52. At the stop sign turn left onto US 52-42. Travel 4.2 miles and turn right on SR 42. Proceed 10.2 miles and turn right on CR 625. At 0.4 miles bear to the right where there is a "Y" in the road. Travel 7.6 miles to FS 631 and turn right on this road. Travel 2.6 miles up the mountain to an earth barrier. This is the parking area. One note of caution. FS 631 is a rough road and requires a vehicle with a high wheel base. From this parking area one can hike in several directions.

Trail Description

This easy trail winds slowly down to Roaring Fork. There are campsites down near the creek. The trail passes through large rhododendron thickets and beautiful stands of hardwoods. Large hickory, oak, hemlock, and even frazier magnolia can be seen.

The trail crosses two earth dikes. Be careful here as there is a trench between the two dikes. There is also a Forest Service information center in this area. The trail is an old road. At approximately 0.1 miles is the junction with the Chestnut Ridge Trail (See Chestnut Ridge Trail description). The Roaring Fork Connector Trail travels straight through this intersection. A right on the Chestnut Ridge Trail goes up the mountain to the AT, while a left goes down the mountain to another access into the Beartown Wilderness Area.

Initially, the trail has a very gentle climb but quickly begins a slow descent to Roaring Fork. The trail contours along the mountain, weaving in and out of small shoulders and hollows. Just prior to reaching the creek, the forest changes from oak-hickory to species found along the creek bottoms. Hemlock, poplar, and an occasional Frazier magnolia can be seen. At the creek, there are several nice campsites.

The trail moves upstream a short distance. About one hundred yards from the first clearing is another trail which leads down the fork (See Roaring Fork Trail description). The trail leading up the fork plays out quickly. However, there is a small waterfall where Cove Branch drains into Roaring Fork. Just past the junction of the two creeks is the best access to the top of Garden Mountain (See Garden Mountain Bushwhack description).

When hiking, remember to pack out your trash.

James
River
Face
Wilderness

James River Face

James River Face Wilderness is located in Rockbridge and Bedford Counties, about thirteen miles south of Lexington, Virginia. The wilderness area is in the Glenwood Ranger District of the Jefferson National Forest and encompasses an area of approximately 8,903 acres. It is one of the largest wilderness areas in Virginia. James River Face was declared a wilderness in 1984.

James River Face is located on the northern end of Thunder Ridge, a long ridge in the Blue Ridge Mountains. On the north, the wilderness is bordered by the James River. Along the southern border runs Forest Service road 95. The Blue Ridge Parkway forms the eastern border. This primitive area includes both eastern and western slopes of the Blue Ridge Mountains. There are no major creeks within the James River Face Wilderness; therefore, it is best to pack water when hiking through the area.

The trail system throughout the wilderness is extensive. The wilderness has approximately twenty-seven miles of trails which are generally well maintained with few natural barriers. There is only one trail in the wilderness area which is not maintained. This old road exits Thunder Ridge wilderness to enter the James River Face Wilderness. It is not officially maintained but is nevertheless in excellent condition. Except for the southern end of the Appalachian Trail, the trails begin at the base of the mountain and climb to ridge crests. This characteristic may be a deterrent to some, but the hiking is excellent.

The ecosystem of the James River Face is dominated by the oak-hickory forest. There are, however, scattered pockets of white pine, hemlock, chestnut oak, and Virginia pine. Much of the Virginia pine in the James River Face has been affected by the Southern Pine Bark Beetle and is dead or dying. The hemlock rust blister has purchased a foothold within the wilderness boundary and is affecting hemlock populations.

There are several areas of interest within the James River Face Wilderness. Devils Marble Yard is notable for its numerous large boulders. This intriguing site encompasses several acres along Belfast Trail and showcases boulders that are often larger than a school bus. Another area of interest is Marble Spring. This small spring is located just off of the Appalachian Trail near Highcock Knob. At 3,900 feet, Highcock Knob is the highest point in the James River Face. The summit is easy to reach via the Appalachian Trail's southern trailhead. The summit is well worth the trip as the vistas to the

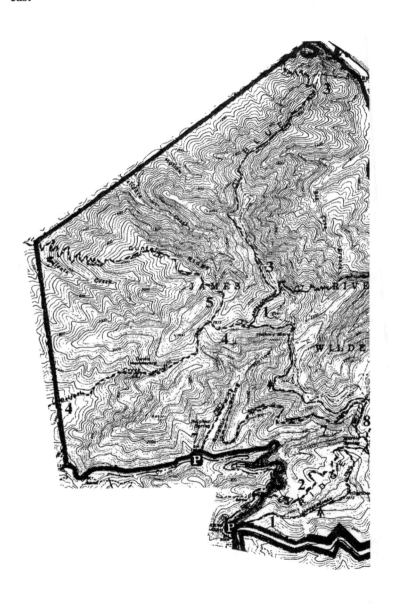

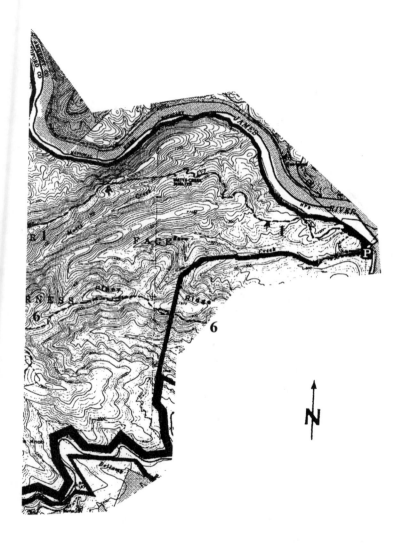

and west are breathtaking. Another point of interest is for the bold adventurer. Although difficult to reach, the land along the James River is rugged, beautiful, and filled with treasures for the intrepid hiker.

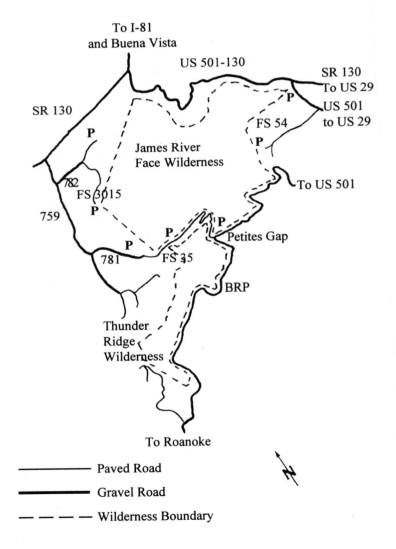

Appalachian Trail   1

Length: 9.9 Miles (One Way)
Time: 6 Hours
Elevation Change: 2,400 Feet
Difficulty: Very Difficult
USGS Map: Snowden
Trailhead: US 130 and FS 35

How To Get There

Take I-81 to Exit #180. Take US 11 South 3.5 miles to SR 130.
Turn left on SR 130 and proceed 12.6 miles. Turn left on US 501.
Proceed 0.2 miles to a parking area on the right.

From Lynchburg, take US 29 and turn west on SR 130. Proceed
12.5 miles to US 501. Turn left on US 501 and cross the James
River. Proceed 0.3 miles to a parking area on the right.

To reach the upper parking area, take the BRP to milepost 71 at
Petites Gap. Turn onto FS 35 and proceed 0.1 miles to parking area
on the right.

Trail Description

The trail begins at the parking area described above. Shortly
after beginning the hike, there is a James River Face Wilderness sign
and a Forest Service information center. For the first 1.5 miles the
trail exhibits a series of gentle slopes. There are frequent views of
the James River Valley to the right. To the northeast, Peavine Mountain rises high above the river bottom. At appoximately 1.5 miles,
the trail turns left and travels around a bend. At 2.0 miles, there is
another left and the trail passes through some rocks. At about 2.5
miles, the trail reaches a stream. As the trail nears the creek, there
will be some rock steps leading down to the Matts Creek shelter
which is a short walk ahead. The Matts Creek Shelter is a pleasant
place to rest and filter water as the trail soon starts up the mountain.

Just past the shelter, cross the stream via a man-made bridge.
There is a right, then a left switchback followed by a long, moderate
uphill grade. The crest of the finger ridge is reached at the 3.5 mile
mark. To the right there are several rocks and an overlook. From
this overlook, the town of Glasgow and the House Mountains are
visible (See picture, p. 55). The trail follows the ridge crest. At 4.25
miles, the trail drops off the crest to the north side of the mountain.

A view from the Appalachian Trail

The vegetation changes quickly as mountain laurel and rhododendron crowd the understory. The trail contours the mountainside for a short distance and then resumes its uphill course.

As the trail swings around the side of the ridge, the valley to the right rises. Hemlock become prevalent as the stream gets closer to trail level. At the stream crossing, stop for a rest as a tough uphill will follow. After crossing the stream, there is a series of approximately ten switchbacks, and the trail moves rapidly up the mountain. This is a particularly grueling section of trail. After completing the switchsbacks, a wide "S" turn puts the down side of the ridge to the hiker's right. Following this grueling climb is an easy uphill grade. After a left-handed turn, the AT reaches the intersection with the Balcony Falls Trail (See Balcony Falls Trail description). The Balcony Falls Trail exits to the right. This intersection is at the 5.5 mile mark.

Follow the sign that points in the direction of the AT. After another 0.5 miles of contouring the AT reaches the intersection with the Belfast Trail (See Belfast Trail description). At this junction, the AT goes to the left and the Belfast Trail exits the AT to the right. There is a small campsite at this junction surrounded by several large oaks and small chestnuts. The AT starts downhill after this junction. The grade is very gentle and the trail is well maintained. There are beautiful views to the south, mostly of Thunder Ridge. Pine and chestnut oak are the dominant species in this dry area. Many of the pines are dead, however, having fallen victim to the Southern Pine Bark Beetle. There are many blueberry plants along the trail, too.

After the descent, the trail starts an easy uphill climb through laurel and small hemlock. The trail winds around a shoulder of the mountain and starts downhill again. There is a small open area with a small trail to the left. This trail leads to an old road which travels across the ridge top. The trail passes another small clearing with a campsite. The trail bends to the left and then there is a trail junction with the Sulphur Spring Trail and the Piney Ridge Trail. The signs at this junction identify the Piney Ridge Horse Trail and outline distances to nearby landmarks including Malt Creek Trail (5.1 miles), Snowden Bridge (7.7 miles), Petites Gap (2.75 miles), Marble Spring (0.5 miles), and water (0.25 miles).

After this junction the trail starts a long slow descent to Marble Spring. The trail passes through a forest of small pines and hardwoods. There is a switch to the right and then a long straight stretch to the spring. At the gap, there is a junction with the "water" trail (See Water Trail description). This trail exits to the left. Marble Spring is to the right and downhill about 300 feet. There is good camping in this area.

The trail exits Marble Spring and approximately 100 yards later makes a right switchback. The climb is moderate and the trail is clear of bush. At a left switchback is the trail junction for the AT Connector Trail. This junction is about 0.3 miles from Marble Spring. A right leads to the Thunder Ridge Wilderness (See AT Connector Trail description). After the junction the trail enters a flat region and the grade is easy. This easy grade is short and soon the trail begins a steep climb to Highcock Knob.

The climb to the Knob is difficult. After a short, straight incline there are two left switchbacks. These switchbacks help to ease the difficulty of the climb, but only slightly. The summit of Highcock Knob, 3,073 feet, is the highest point in the James River Face Wilderness. The summit is flat and there is a view of the piedmont region of Virginia.

Upon leaving the crest there is a short, steep descent through a forest of chestnut oak. This descent is followed by a short, difficult climb. At the top of this small crest, the trail passes through a forest of small chestnut oak, pine, and mountain laurel. The laurel begins to crowd the trail. Then the trail descends to the FS 35. Initially, this descent is steep, but the grade becomes easy when the trail enters the Petites Gap area. In Petites Gap the smaller chestnut oak give way to much larger red oak, white oak, and tulip poplar. Just before FS 35, the trail passes a small wilderness sign. There is a Forest Service information center at the parking area on FS 35.

AT Connector Trail   2

Length: 1.3 Miles
Time: 45 Minutes
Difficulty: Easy
Elevation Change: 360 Feet
USGS Maps: Snowden
Trailhead: FS 35

How To Get There

Take I-81 to Exit #180. Take US 11 South 3.5 miles to SR 130. Turn left on SR 130 and proceed 3.2 miles to CR 759. Turn right on CR 759 and travel 3.2 miles. Turn left on CR 781. The parking area is located 0.1 miles from the intersection of FS 35 and the BRP. The trailhead is located approximately 0.5 miles down FS 35.

From Lynchburg, take SR 130 to the BRP. Travel South on the BRP to Petites Gap near milepost 71. Turn right on FS 35 and travel 0.1 miles to a parking area on the right. The trailhead is located about 0.5 miles down FS 35.

Trail Description

This trail is a continuation of the Horse Trail located in the Thunder Ridge Wilderness Area (See Thunder Ridge Wilderness: Horse Trail on FS 35 description). This trail is an easy hike along an old road cut into the side of the mountain. The Horse Trail exits FS 35 approximately 0.4 miles from the Petites Gap parking area. Traveling downhill leads to the Thunder Ridge Wilderness. Hiking uphill leads into the James River Face Wilderness.

The trail crosses over an old earth barrier and begins to climb. The grade is easy as the trail follows the contours of the mountain. The area is covered with gnarly, old chestnut oak. After a bend to the right, the trail enters a sheltered area where some of the oaks grow to very large proportions. At the end of the bowl, the trail bends to the left. The land becomes drier and the trees change from a mixed-hardwood forest to a forest of small pine and oak. Mountain laurel makes up much of the ground cover. The grade remains easy.

Approximately 0.5 miles after the bend, the trail forks. The left fork is a road which is brush-covered and difficult to follow. The right fork begins to climb, and the trail becomes a footpath. Shortly after this fork, the trail connects with the AT. A left proceeds to Marble Spring and a right leads to Highcock Knob and back to Petites Gap (See AT description).

The moon over Devil's Marble Yard.

Balcony Falls Trail   3

Length: 4.5 miles
Time: 2.5 Hours
Elevation Change: 1,850 feet
Difficulty: Difficult
USGS Maps: Snowden
Trailhead: FS 3093

<u>How To Get There</u>

Take I-81 to Exit #180. Take US 11 South 3.5 miles to SR 130. Turn left on SR 130 and proceed 3.2 miles to CR 759. Turn right on 759 and travel 0.8 miles. Turn left on CR 782. Proceed 1.7 miles to the parking area.

From Lynchburg, take US 29 and turn west on SR 130 and proceed 29 miles. After crossing the mountain near Glasgow, SR 130 turns left. Turn left on CR 759 and follow the above directions.

Trail Description

The Balcony Falls Trail is a pleasant climb from the James River to the top of an unnamed ridge. After cresting the ridge, the trail intersects with the A.T. The climb is steady but contains many switchbacks. There are many views of the surrounding area to both the northwest and the southeast. The trail can be coupled with the Gunters Ridge Trail for an approximated 13 mile circuit.

From the parking area on FS 3093, the trail begins at the Forest Service information center. It crosses a fence, makes a right, and a small sign provides directions. The trail passes through a small meadow until reaching another sign and information center. This information center should have a USGS map of the James River Face Wilderness Area. For the first mile or so, the path has a gradual descent. Enjoy this while it lasts.

At about 1.0 miles the trail begins its ascent of the ridge. The trail begins by meandering upward. A series of switchbacks (22 in all) climbs to the crest of the ridge. Along the way, there are many pines which have been damaged by the Southern Pine Bark Beetle, an insect that is devastating pine forests in Virginia.

Three miles into the hike, the crest of the ridge is attained and there is a beautiful view of the valley below. The next section of the trail follows the ridge to the summit. The views from this trail are spectacular and instill a feeling of being on top of the world. The trail is bordered by small hardwoods, and the colors of the fall foilage are stunning.

The next milestone is a sign that reads "AT 1 1/2." Shortly after this sign, the trail descends slightly to the right of the ridgetop. The soil quality diminishes and small pitch pine dominate the forest. At about 5.0 miles there is another sign that reads "Saw Mill Hollow." At 6.0 miles there is a campsite (no water) and a left-handed switchback. The intersection with the AT is about 0.25 miles beyond this switchback. At the intersection, there is a sign indicating the direction of the AT. Branching away from the AT and contouring across the ridge is the Sulfur Springs Trail. Following the AT across the ridge to the right takes the hiker to a junction with the Belfast and Gunters Ridge Trails. Following the Gunters Ridge Trail, coupled with a short hike down CR 759, makes a pleasant circuit hike. Following the AT to the left and down the mountain will take the hiker about 5.0 miles to the Snowden Bridge and US 501.

Belfast Trail 4

Length: 3.0 Miles (One Way)
Time: 2 Hours
Elevation Change: 1,700 Feet
Difficulty: Moderately Difficult
USGS Map: Snowden
Trailhead: CR 781

How To Get There

Take I-81 to Exit #180. Take US 11 South 3.5 miles to SR 130. Turn left on SR 130 and proceed 3.2 miles to CR 759. Turn right on 759, travel 3.2 miles, and turn left on CR 781. Travel 1.3 miles to the trailhead.

From Lynchburg, take US 29 and turn west on SR 130 and proceed miles to 29 miles. After crossing the mountain, near Glasgow, SR 130 turns left. Turn left on CR 759 and follow the above directions.

Trail Description

The Belfast Trail leads to the top of the ridge and eventually connects with the AT. The trail is well-maintained and very easy to follow. Along the way, the trail passes the aptly named Devils Marble Yard, a large granite boulder field stretching up the side of the mountain. It is possible to spend an entire day exploring all the nooks and crannies among the boulders. The trail passes through areas of cove hardwoods. Near the peak, the forests are dominated by oak and hickory.

The trail begins by crossing a bridge and a sign posting distances. Devils Marble Yard is 1.0 miles, the Gunter Ridge Trail is 2.0 miles, and the AT is 3.0 miles. Belfast Trail is marked with blue blazes. Just after crossing the bridge are two stone columns with the words "Camp Powhatan." A little farther down the trail, there is an orange blazed trail which crosses the Belfast Trail. There are some campsites near this trail crossing. The trail maintains a very easy grade for the first 0.5 miles.

The trail passes the remains of several old buildings and then crosses a small branch. There is another trail marked with orange blazes which exits to the left. The grade of the trail becomes more moderate through this area. Finally, the James River Face Wildeness

Morning sun in the James River Face.

sign is reached in a region dominated by small mixed hardwoods, pine, laurel and dogwood.

At 0.7 miles the trail crosses a small creek. A pleasant campsite is located on the left. After two more creek crossings, the trail grade becomes moderate and is lined with beautiful ferns and large cove hardwoods. Tulip poplar, sassafras, hickory, and oak are seen in large numbers.

The trail becomes very steep and Devils Marble Yard can be seen on the left. There is a small waterfall on the right. Just beyond the waterfall is a short trail to the left leading to Devils Marble Yard. Above Devils Marble Yard, the trail grade becomes more moderate.

The trail passes through a small gap and becomes more flat. A small trail to the right leads to a campsite. This campsite is about 1.5 miles from the trailhead. The trail begins to climb to another flat area and the junction with the Gunter Ridge Trail (See Gunter Ridge Trail description). At the junction is a nice campsite with large old oaks and a sign. The sign designates the following distances: the Gunter Ridge Trailhead, 4.0 miles and the AT, 0.5 miles.

The trail continues with a easy grade. The Belfast Trail then meets the AT (See AT description). There is a sign with distances to the Gunter Ridge Trail and the Devils Marble Yard, 0.5 miles and 1.25 miles, respectively. There is a nice spot to camp in this area beneath an imposing stand of large oak. The Belfast Trail when connected with the Sulphur Spring Trail and a walk down FS 35, make a nice loop hike.

Gunter Ridge Trail 5

Length: 5.5 Miles (One Way)
Time: 3.5 Hours
Elevation Change: 1,560 Feet
Difficulty: Difficult
USGS Maps: Snowden
Trailhead: FS 54

How To Get There:

Take I-81 to Exit #180. Take US 11 South 3.5 miles to SR 130.
Turn left on SR 130 and proceed 3.2 miles to CR 759. Turn right on
759 and travel 0.8 miles. Turn left on CR 782. Proceed 1.1 miles to
the junction with FS 3093 and turn right. Continue 0.5 miles to
aparking area on the right.

From Lynchburg, take US 29 and turn west on SR 130 and proceed 29 miles. Turn left on CR 759 and follow the above directions.

Trail Description:

The Gunter Ridge Trail is a pleasant hike that is most suitably
included in a circuit hike when combined with the Balcony Falls
Trail. An "in-out" hike on the Gunter Ridge Trail is not recommended due to the lack of anything extremely outstanding to see
(i.e. 9 miles of this trail would quickly become boring). The trail
starts on an old forest road and then travels up the mountain to intersect with Belfast Trail. The trail is an excellent route for access to
the AT.

From the gate that blocks the road, travel down the road about
1.25 miles to a sign. This road will pass behind some private dwell-
ings. The wilderness area is to the left of the road. At the sign take
a left and begin an easy uphill grade. There will be a "Y" intersection at about 3 miles. Take another left at this intersection. Be very
careful here because the path to the right appears more worn. A
wrong turn may be made if not cautious. After making this left the
trail becomes rocky and crosses a small stream.

From the stream, the trail continues up and passes a wilderness
sign at the 4.5 mile mark. After this sign, the trail begins to climb
Gunter Ridge. There is a series of 15 or so switchbacks. After the
switchbacks, the trail continues to climb at a moderate grade to the
junction with Belfast Trail. There is a sign at this intersection point-

ing back down Gunter Ridge. To get to the intersection with the AT, take a left. This is Belfast Trail and it follows across the top of the ridge for about 0.5 miles and ends at the juncton (See Belfast Trail description).

Piney Ridge Trail   6

Length: 3.0 Miles (One Way)
Time: 1.5 Hours
Elevation Change: 1,720 Feet
Difficulty: Difficult
USGS Map: Snowden
Trailhead: FS 54

How To Get There

Take I-81 to Exit #180. Take US 11 South 3.5 miles to SR 130. Turn left on SR 130 and proceed 12.9 miles to US 501. Turn right on US 501 and cross the James River. Proceed 1.4 miles and turn right on FS 54. Watch closely for the road. Travel 0.5 miles and turn right on a small gravel road with a sign for the Piney Ridge Trail. The parking area is 0.1 miles from the intersection.

From US 29, turn West on SR 130 and proceed 19.6 miles to US 501. Turn left on US 501, and cross the James River. Then follow the above directions

Trail Description

The Piney Ridge Trail is a pleasant, albeit plain, walk from FS 54 to the top of Piney Ridge where it intersects with the AT and Sulfur Springs Trail. The trail is fairly difficult. The majority of the walk is a combination of intermediate and difficult uphill climbs. The path follows an old fire road which is slowly being reclaimed by nature. The closer to the crest of the ridge, the more nature has reclaimed.

From the gate on the fire road, walk about one hundred feet and look for the trail to the right. The road begins to bend left and the trail branches off between some pines to the right. There is a sign at the trailhead that reads "Appalachian Trail 3 1/2." Initially, the grade is easy to moderate, but this changes quickly.

At first, the trail follows an overgrown logging road. The timber adjacent to the road is young and even aged, suggesting that timber was harvested in the not too distant past. At about one mile, there is a series of four switchbacks and then a wilderness boundary marker. The switches are at the moderate to difficult level as is the majority of the remainder of the trail.

From the wilderness sign the trail continues up the mountain. There are a few blue and yellow blazes. However, following the trail is not difficult. The trail travels to the left side of the ridge top, through alternating stands of pine then mixed hardwood. The forest canopy opens up as the trail climbs to the crest of the ridge. The walk can be very warm in the heat of the summer sun.

At about three miles the trail intersects with an old fire road. Take a left. After a short walk, the Piney Ridge Trail intersects the AT and Sulfur Spring Trail.

Mushrooms can be found throughout the wilderness areas of Virginia. Be aware that most mushrooms are poisonous and can be deadly if eaten. Never eat mushrooms unless absolutely certain of the variety.

Sulphur Spring Trail   7

Length: 2.7 Miles (One Way)
Time: 1.5 Hours
Elevation Change: 1,050 Feet
Difficulty: Moderate
USGS Map:Snowden
Trailhead: FS 35
How To Get There

Take I-81 to Exit #180. Take US 11 South 3.5 miles to SR 130.
Turn left on SR 130 and proceed 3.2 miles to CR 759. Turn right on
CR 759 and travel 3.2 miles. Turn left on CR 781. Travel 3.1 miles
to the trailhead. CR 781 becomes FS 35 prior to reaching the parking area. The trailhead is located on the left.

From Lynchburg, take SR 130 West. Travel 29 miles to the
intersection CR 759 and turn right. After crossing the mountain,
near Glasgow, SR 130 turns left. Then follow the above directions.

Trail Description

The Sulphur Spring Trail is a short trail which joins the Appalachian and Piney Ridge Trails at the crest of Piney Ridge. It follows
an old road etched in the side of the mountain. The trail begins on
the left side of the road. There is a wilderness sign and a FS information center located at the trailhead. The initial part of the trail is
narrow and poison ivy thrives along the trail's edges. The trail is flat
and easy. About 0.5 miles, the trail bends right and crosses Sulphur
Spring Creek. In this area there are many large hemlocks, white
pines, and poplars.

At the end of the bowl, the trail begins to climb, and the grade
becomes moderate. The forest changes from cove hardwoods and
hemlock to more dry species such as Virginia pine, chestnut oak,
and blueberry. The trail bends left and continues to climb. The trail
bends right and then left again. At 1.8 miles, just beyond this bend
to the left, is a rock outcrop with a great view to the south and east.
This panoramic view highlights the prominant Thunder Ridge. The
grade continues to be moderate. Shortly after this rock outcrop, the
trail reaches the crest of Piney Ridge. Located at the crest is the
junction with Piney Ridge Trail and the AT. There is also a sign
indicating directions to a water source. This water is suitable for
horses but is not fit for human consumption. This trail, when com-

bined with the AT, the Belfast Trail, and a short walk down the FS 35, makes an enjoyable circuit hike.

Water Trail   8

Length: 0.5 Miles
Time: 20 Minutes
Elevation Change:200 Feet
Difficulty: Easy
USGS Map: Snowden
Trailhead: Junction of Sulpher Spring Trail and the AT

How To Get There

This trail is located at the junction of the Sulphur Spring Trail, the AT, and the Piney Ridge Trail.

Trail Description

At the trail junctions described above, the Water Trail heads east climbing to a small muddy pond. There are many small pines and chestnut oaks in this area. The trail bends to the right and begins to descend downhill after the pond. The trail is quite brushy through this downhill section. The trail leads to a saddle at the base of Highcock Knob where it rejoins the AT. There is a nice campsite in this saddle and a spring about 300 feet to the left of the AT.

Kimberling Creek Wilderness

Kimberling Creek

The Kimberling Creek Wilderness is a 5,580 acre area located in the Wythe Ranger District of the Jefferson National Forest. The wilderness receives its name from Kimberling Creek which flows to the southeast of the wilderness. The primitive area is located approximately seventeen miles north of Wytheville, Virginia in the eastern portion of Bland County. Kimberling Creek was declared a wilderness by Congress in 1984.

Kimberling Creek is located on the southern side of Hogback Mountain and includes a long shoulder on the southeastern flank of the mountain. The Hogback Mountain ridge top forms the northern border. Sulphur Spring Creek and Forest Service road 281 form the southern boundary of the wilderness. North Fork, a small creek created by a spring high on Hogback Mountain, is the main drainage within the boundaries of Kimberling Creek Wilderness. This small creek runs through the heart of the wilderness. There are smaller spring fed creeks which drain into the Sulphur Spring Creek at the southern end of the wilderness.

The wilderness is completely undeveloped and there are no maintained trails. The trails described here are the remains of old forgotten roads and an old railroad grade. Many of the hikes are difficult due to the primitive nature of the area. However, this remoteness is also Kimberlings Creek 's major advantage. There are about three miles of old roads within the wilderness boundary. An old railroad grade lies along North Fork and is about three miles in length. The remainder of the hikes are cross-country jouneys which should only be done with a good map and a compass.

The forest of Kimberling Creek Wilderness is comprised of three major types. The first is the shelter coves located within the North Fork drainage as well as along the Sulpher Spring Creek. Here, towering poplar, white pine, and hemlock thrive. Rhododendron and dogwood are found in great abundance. One can even see an occasional paw paw, a tree left behind from the days when Virginia had a more tropical climate. Another major forest type includes the oak-hickory forests common to nearly all Virginia mountains. Kimberling Creek Wilderness is comprised primarily of this type of forest. The size of the trees depends upon the location with some trees growing quite large on the southeastern flank of Hogback Mountain. Finally, a third area is comprised of rhododendron thickets which surround the spring at the headwaters of North Fork. A trip through the thickets can be daunting, but the spring makes the trek worth the effort.

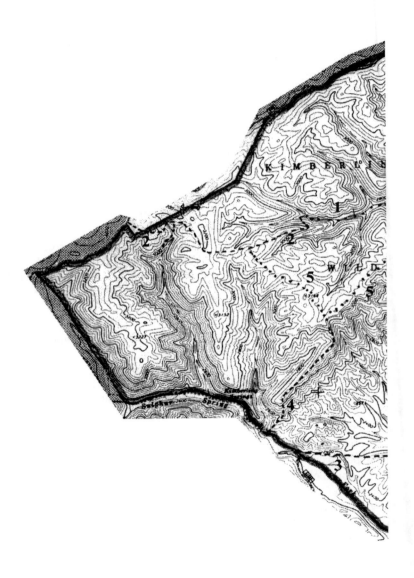

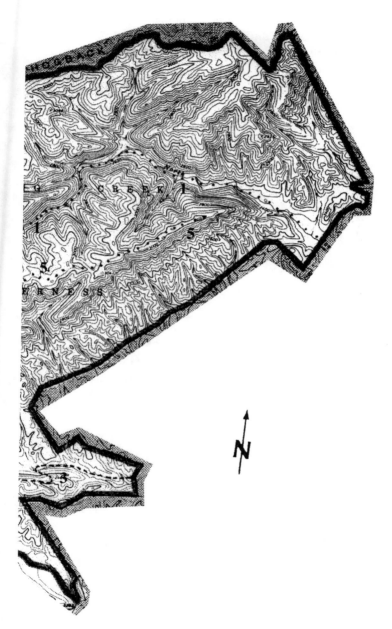

One note of caution about the Kimberling Creek Wilderness Area. The North Fork area has sustained a tremendous amount of storm damage and the hiking is difficult. Further, the area is very remote and a severe injury sustained in this area could prove to be fatal as travel is very difficult. Remember to hike with a friend if you plan to hike/bushwhack through this area.

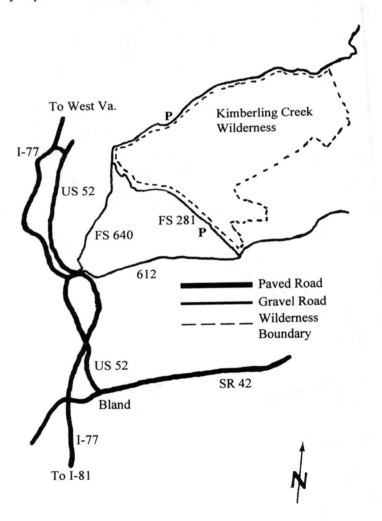

North Fork   1

Length: 3.6 Miles (One Way)
Time: 3.5 Hours
Elevation Change: 700 Feet
Difficulty: Very Difficult
USGS Map: Rocky Gap
Trailhead: FS 640

How To Get There

The North Fork Bushwhack is reached via the Ridgetop Trail.

Trail Description

The North Fork is best accessed from the top of Hogback Mountain via the Ridgetop Trail (See Ridgetop Trail description). This is a rugged area for only the most intrepid hikers. There is a great deal of storm damage throughout the drainage of the North Fork. Although the damage makes hiking more difficult, the area is very beautiful. There are large trees, as well as scenic clifftops. The North Fork is a gentle flowing creek and is generally very shallow. There are many areas where the hiker can actually hike in the creek bed by walking across large flat stones which litter the stream. There is also an old railroad bed along the creek bottom which is evidenced by sections of railroad ties and washed out bridge abutments.

There are several areas appropriate for camping and water is plentiful. Be aware, however, that taking a pack into this remote area could be very difficult. There are areas of storm fall which encompass 150 feet of hiking distance. These sections require either climbing over or crawling under the damage. If you are interested in seeing true wilderness, this is probably the most remote area found in the Virginia wilderness system.

A garter snake on the North Fork.

Ridgetop Trail   2

Length: 1.2 Miles (One Way)
Time: 45 Minutes
Elevation Change: 350 Feet
Difficulty: Easy
USGS Map: Rocky Gap
Trailhead: FS 640

How To Get There

Take I-81 to I-77 North. Take Exit #48 and turn right at the stop sign. Travel 0.8 miles and turn left onto US 52. Travel 3.9 miles and turn right onto CR 612. Travel 0.3 miles and turn left on FS 640. Travel 4.6 miles to a small parking area on the right. The FS road is rough and not recommended for vehicles with low wheel bases.

Trail Description

From the trailhead, an old road leads across the top of the ridge. The road eventually leads to the North Fork and provides the easiest access to the North Fork region of the wilderness. The road is a gentle hike to the vicinity of the North Fork. Here the trail begins a very rapid descent to the creek.

The trail begins at the top of Hogback Mountain and descends to the North Fork. The forest species near the top include chestnut oak, hickory, maple, and white pine. A short distance from the FS road, there is a small sign indicating the entrance into the Kimberling Creek Wilderness. There is also a small earthen barrier near the sign. Just beyond the sign is a small road to the right, which dies out after about 0.25 of a miles. The road drops gradually for about 1.5 miles then drops rapidly to the North Fork.

After a switchback to the left, the forest changes to cove hardwoods, hemlock, and white pine. There are also many large rhododendron in this area. After the switchback, the trail drops rapidly then levels out near the creek. Once at the creek turning left leads to the headwaters of the North Fork. A right turn heads down the North Fork. Either direction is a bushwhack.

Sulphur Spring Trail   3

Length: 1.6 Miles (One way)
Time: 45 Minutes
Elevation Change: 150 Feet
Difficulty: Easy
USGS Map: Rocky Gap
Trailhead: FS 281

How To Get There

Take I-81 to I-77 North. Take Exit #48 and turn right at the stop sign. Travel 0.8 miles and turn left onto US 52. Travel 3.9 miles and turn right on CR 612. Travel 3.9 miles and turn left on FS 281. Proceed 1.0 mile to a parking area on the left. Remember, do not to block the gate.

Trail Description

This trail, a short "out and back," is actually an old road into the lower southern corner of the wilderness area. To reach the trailhead, hike up FS 281about 50 yards, and after crossing the creek, look for the trailhead on the right. The trail follows a gentle contour along the Sulphur Spring Fork. There is some storm damage along the trail, but it is not impossible to get around. There are many nice spots in this area for camping.

After approximately 0.5 miles, the trail crosses over a small ridge and drops down into another small creek drainage. The trail bends gradually to the right and begins to follow a dry stream bed. This trail eventually joins another road about 0.25 miles outside the wilderness boundary.

The main forest species in this area are large white pine and hemlock. Oak, maple, and hickory are also present.

Trail To The Ridge   4

Length: 1 Mile (One Way)
Time: 45 Minutes
Elevation Change: 720 Feet
Difficulty: Moderate
USGS Map: Rocky Gap
Trailhead: FS 281

How to Get There

Take I-81 to I-77 North. Take Exit #48 and turn right at the stop sign. Travel 0.8 miles and turn left onto US 52. Travel 3.9 miles and turn right on CR 612. Travel 3.9 miles and turn left on FS 281. Proceed 1.0 mile to a parking area on the left. Remember, do not block the gate. The trailhead is located in a small field approximately 0.4 miles farther up the road.

Trail Description

This trail shows only light use and at times is indistinct and hard to follow. Once the ridge top is reached, the trail soon disappears altogether. Although difficult to follow, this trail provides quick access to the ridge top where there are many hiking possibilities. All of the possibilities require a good contour map and compass.

The trail begins in a small grassy meadow on the right side of the road and climbs up the shoulder of the mountain. The area has many white pine, hemlock, and cove hardwoods such as tulip poplar

A mountain view

and oak. The climb to the ridge, which is steep and steady, begins almost immediately. There is a brief flat section midway through the climb. As the trail rises up the ridge, the forest changes from cove hardwoods and hemlock to the drier species such as chestnut oak, pitch pine, and hickory. Near the top, the oaks and hickory become much larger.

Ridge Top 5

Upon reaching the ridge top, there is a pleasant walk along the ridge to the northeast. Bear left at the ridge top. The crest of the ridge is fairly open and easily traveled. The hike across the ridge is a series of short ups and downs with a gradual decline in elevation. There are panoramic views to the east. At one point, the ridge crest becomes indistinct. In this area, bear to the right and the views to the east again reappear. The ridge becomes very narrow just before the drop to the North Fork. It is easy to tell where the ridge ends as the drop is very abrupt. There are some nice spots to camp near the end of the ridge; however, there is no water.

Lewis
Fork
Wilderness

Lewis Fork

The Lewis Fork Wilderness is one of the best places to hike in the State of Virginia. This wilderness has it all including boggy areas, high upland meadow, huge boulder fields, a spruce-fir forest and the highest point in the state. Lewis Fork is located in the counties of Grayson and Smythe, about twelve miles south of Marion, Virginia. Situated in the Jefferson National Forest, this primitive area occupies a total 5,730 acres. It was declared a wilderness in 1984.

Lewis Fork Wilderness is a scenic area which offers the hiker many rewards. The wilderness area itself is located on the western slope of Pine Mountain and encompasses Mount Rogers, the highest point in the State. The elevations for this roadless area range from 3,280 feet to 5,729 feet. The area spawns many springs which give birth to many creeks including Helton Creek, Lewis Fork, and Grassy Branch. Thus, water is available on most lower altitude trails. Filterable water is scarce at higher altitudes. In the grassy meadows the boulder fields hidden by forested slopes are very visible. These boulder fields are truly spectacular sights.

There are many trails in the Lewis Fork Wilderness. The area offers over thirty miles of trails. Trail circuits of almost any length can be created with varying degrees of difficulty. The Appalachian Trail passes through the Lewis Fork Wilderness and the nearby Little Wilson Creek Wilderness as well as Greyson Highlands State Park. By utilizing the Appalachian Trail one has access to a vast amount of hiking in one area of Virginia.

The forest system of the Lewis Fork is one of the most unique in the Commonwealth. The Mount Rogers summit is the home of frazier fir and red spruce as well as yellow birch. These three species of trees are holdovers from the last ice age and continue to exist in Virginia only because of the high elevations of Mount Rogers. The rest of the western slope is covered mainly by red and sugar maple. Sugar maple is another species which prefers higher elevations in the southerern states. The sheltered coves of the Lewis Fork give rise to large hemlock, tulip poplar, and an occasional beech. The eastern side of the Lewis Fork Wilderness is open meadow. These meadows support such species as mountain ash and chokecherry. Black raspberry is also very common.

One note about unusual wildlife: wild horses inhabit the meadows along the eastern boundary of the Lewis Fork Wilderness. Although the horses are fenced out of the wilderness, many of the trails

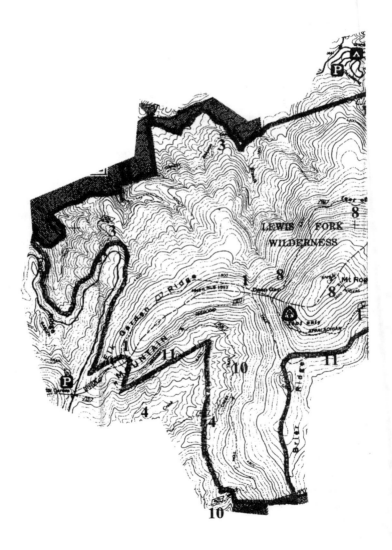

wander in and out of the meadows. During almost any hike, it is possible to see some of the horses that roam wild in the upland meadows.

There are many dangers when hiking at the elevations found in and around Lewis Fork. Most of the wilderness lies above 4,000 feet. At these elevations it is best to be prepared. Weather can change quickly and dramatically. It is far better to be over prepared than under prepared. Remember to bring warm clothing and rain gear in case the weather should turn for the worse.

One final note of caution: Lewis Fork is a favored hunting area. When hiking in the fall or early winter blaze orange should be worn.

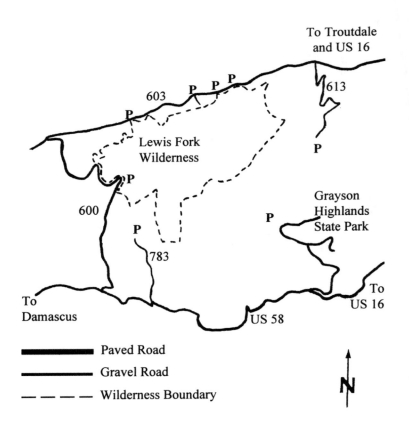

Appalachian Trail   1

Length: 18.0 Miles (One Way)
Time: All Day (Maybe More)
Elevation Change: 2,050 Feet
Difficulty: Very Difficult
USGS Map: White Top Mountain, Troutdale
Trailhead: CR 603, CR 600 and Grayson Highlands State Park

How To Get There

Take I-81 to Marion, Va. Take Exit #45 and turn south on US 16. Travel 17.2 miles and turn right on CR 603. Proceed 9.4 miles and turn left on CR 600. After 100 yards CR 600 turns left again. Travel 5.3 miles to the top of the mountain. Parking is on the right.

Take I-81 to Marion, Va. Take Exit #45 and turn south on US 16. Travel 17.2 miles and turn right on CR 603. Proceed 4.0 miles to a parking area on the left side of the road. The trailhead is located in this parking area.

The other access is at Massies Gap in the Grayson Highlands State Park. The park is located just off US 58 about 7.6 miles west from the intersections of US 16 and US 58. At the park entrance, turn right and follow the signs to Massie's Gap.

Trail Description

In this region the AT passes through the Lewis Fork Wilderness, Little Wilson Creek Wilderness, and Grayson Highlands State Park. It is a beautiful trail that wanders though lowland hardwood forests, upland meadows, and spruce-fir forests. It is easy to follow as it is clearly marked with white blazes. The condition of the trail is excellent. There are many excellent views, primarily to the east and south. There is ample water along the trail, but remember to purify it before drinking. The trail begins off of CR 603 and ends 18 miles later on CR 600. If planning a thorough hike, it is recommended to have a car at the other end.

At the parking area on CR 603, there is a Forest Service information center. The trail enters the woods to the right of the information center. There is a campsite on the left side of the trail just beyond some trash cans and a trail register box. After passing the register, the trail crosses a small bridge, bends to the right, and moves away from the creek. After the bend, the grade changes from easy to moderate. The trees are tall and the forest is dominated by maples with occasional Frazier magnolia and their big wide leaves.

The trail bends left and enters another small creek drainage. The grade becomes easier and the trail parallels this small creek for a short distance. The trail bends right leaving this second creek behind and enters the Lewis Fork Wilderness. There is a sign at the boundary. After about 0.75 miles, the AT crosses the Old Orchard Trail (See Old Orchard Trail description). At the junction, the AT continues straight up the shoulder of the mountain. The grade is still moderate, and the climb is steady. There is a switchback to the left, and then the AT again crosses the Old Orchard Trail.

After crossing this trail, the AT reaches the Old Orchard Trail Shelter. The shelter is 1.5 miles from the trailhead. There is a picnic table at the shelter, and water can be found to the right of the shelter. There is a nice meadow at the shelter and the sugar maples in the area are beautiful. The AT exits the shelter area left of a lean-to and enters a small area of large hemlock. After the hemlock, the AT crosses a small creek 3 times. After each crossing there is a switchback. The grade is moderate after the shelter.

After a left bend, about 2.4 miles from the trailhead, the boundary to the Lewis Fork Wilderness is reached. After exiting the wilderness the trail becomes increasingly wet and rocky. At a large boulder, the trail bends right and enters a wet boggy area covered by with large ferns. There are also many small springs in this area. This area seems to mark the transition zone from lowland hardwoods to yellow birch and red spruce. After a right bend the AT climbs to the upland meadows on the top of Pine Mountain.

At the top of the mountain, a distance of 3.3 miles, there is a sign marking the elevation at 5,000 feet. There is also a trail junction and the old AT exits left. A sign gives the distance to Mt. Rogers: 3.25 miles. The AT continues straight and there is a sign showing the distance to Scales as 1.25 miles. The AT goes through a livestok gate and turns left. The grade is easy. At this pount Crest Horse Trail is straight ahead. There are some large boulders in the meadows and some excellent campsites. After about 0.25 miles, the AT crosses another gate and reenters the woods. Just beyond the gate, the trail starts to descend. The grade is moderate. There is a switchback to the left followed by a switchback to the right. After the switchbacks, the trail crosses several small creeks. Following the creek crossings,
the trail begins to climb again. There are two campsites on the left side of the trail. The trail crosses a gate and enters the Scales area.

A high mountain meadow.

There is a horse corral and information center at Scales. Scales is about 4.1 miles from the beginning of the trail.

On the other side of the horse trail is a sign for State Park, 3 miles and Massies Gap, 5.5 miles. The trail climbs through a big meadow. The grade is moderate and the view is beautiful. After topping the ridge, the AT descends to another livestock gate and enters the woods. At 5.5 miles, the AT crosses the Bearpen Trail (See Little Wilson Creek Wilderness: Bearpen Trail description) and enters the Little Wilson Creek Wilderness. Maples dominate the overstory and ferns cover the ground. The area is wet, especially during spring and rainy periods. After crossing three small creeks, the trail begins to climb at a moderate grade. It levels out for a short distance and then begins a short, difficult descent through an area of loose gravel and stone. The trail becomes an old road and the grade is an easy descent. There are several large maples in this section. Just before the gate, the AT exits the Little Wilson Creek Wilderness. It exits the wilderness approximately 7 miles from the trailhead.

After the gate is a clearing and a junction with the Scales Trail (See Scales Trail description). The AT turns right on the Scales Trail and then makes an immediate left. After crossing a small bridge and a road, the AT climbs some steps to a flat area. There will be a section of stones to cross. The trail enters a small clearing and drops down to Big Wilson Creek. After crossing the creek, a stile goes over a fence and the AT enters the Grayson Highlands State Park. Once in the park, the trail begins an easy ascent through a field and then enters the woods. After entering the woods, the AT climbs to an old road and turns left. Once on the road, the trail travels over another stile and parallels a fence. There are several small creek crossings and then another fence crossing. The trail then drops quickly to Quebec Creek. This creek crossing is about 7.9 miles from the trailhead.

After crossing the creek, the grade becomes more steep and difficult. After a switchback to the right and then one to the left, the trail enters a wet region. The trail also becomes rocky. The AT exits the woods and enters an area of low shrubs and trees. The grade becomes moderate. Finally, the AT breaks out into a large meadow covered with tremendous boulders. This is Wilburn Ridge and it is 9.1 miles from the trailhead. The view is spectacular. The trail wraps around a huge bowl and the grade is easy. On the left side of the bowl the AT crosses a horse trail at Massies Gap. The gap is reached at 10.6 miles. There is a sign here for AT with northern distances to Scales, 5.0 miles and Old Orchard Shelter, 8.1 miles. Distances south are Rhododendron Gap, 2.1 miles; Thomas Knob Shelter, 2.9 miles; and Mt. Rogers, 3.8 miles. The AT crosses a horse trail and continues to climb around the end of the bowl.

At the next trail junction about .75 miles from Massies Gap, the trail crosses another stile, exits the Grayson Highlands State Park, and enters the Mount Rogers National Recreation Area. The AT crosses the Virginia Highlands Horse Trail and continues its climb. Here the grade becomes steep and the trail is very rocky. The Wilburn Ridge Trail exits left and climbs over the mountain. The Wilburn Ridge Trail is approximately 12 miles from the starting point. The AT skirts right of the peak and then begins to drop. At one point it travels through a crevice in the rocks and the temperature drops slightly in this cool, shady area. The Wilburn Ridge Trail reconnects with the AT on the opposite side of the small peak. Once on the east side of the peak, the evergreen covered top of Mount Rogers is visible.

The AT climbs again to another set of rocks and drops down into the Rhododendron gap. At the gap is a sign for the Lewis Fork Wilderness. There is also a sign for the distance to Mount Rogers, 1.75 miles and Scales, via the Pine Mountain Trail, 3 miles. The gap itself is about 12.7 miles from CR 603. The AT crosses the Crest Horse Trail and then parallels the wilderness boundary to the Thomas Knob Shelter. The grade is easy and the trail weaves in and out of the meadows and the spruce fir forest. There are many campsites in this area. The meadow in this region is covered with black raspberry bushes. The trail descends at a moderate rate just before reaching the Thomas Knob Shelter. There is a privy at the shelter, and the area looks as if it is suffering from serious overuse.

The trail continues to drop for a short distance after the shelter and then begins to climb again. The ascent is easy. The AT crosses another gate and re-enters the Lewis Fork Wilderness. The AT reaches the wilderness at 14 miles. The next landmark is the junction with the Mount Rogers Summit Trail. The summit trail exits to the right (See Mount Rogers Trail description). After the summit trail, the AT descends at a moderate rate. The meadow again is covered with black raspberries. Mountain ash and chokecherry trees are scattered across the meadow.

The trail enters the woods at a wet area, crossing many small streams. The grade is a moderate descent. During this descent the spruce and yellow birch give way to maple. The trail begins to climb again at a moderate rate and comes to a clearing. The AT turns right and climbs again. At a clearing there is a fence on the left. The fence can be crossed by using the stile. While climbing, the spruce again becomes the dominant species. Next, the trail begins a long descent to the junction with the Mount Rogers Trail. The trail grade becomes difficult and very rocky. There will be a switchback to the left and then one to the right. The spruce again gives way to the maples. After the switchbacks the grade becomes moderate and the quality of the trail improves.

The Mount Rogers Trail enters the AT from the right. There is a sign for Grindstone Campground and Elk Garden at the junction. The trail junction is 14.8 miles from the trailhead. The AT turns left onto a road and continues to descend. The trail enters Deep Gap on Elk Garden Ridge. Camping is prohibited in this area because of overuse. The Virginia Highlands Horse Trail passes through this gap to the left of the AT. On the other side of the gap, the AT bends right and begins to climb. The grade is moderate and the climb is not long. When the trail bends left, the grade becomes easy as the trail meanders along the west side of Elk Garden Ridge.

About 0.9 miles from Deep Gap, there is a rock outcrop with views to the southwest. At this outcrop, the trail turns left and heads down the mountain. The grade is moderate and the trail is rocky. When the angle of descent decreases, there is another gate and the AT exits Lewis Fork Wilderness. This gate is 17.3 miles from the trailhead. Go through the gate and head to the meadow. This takes the hiker to CR 600 and the end of the trek, approximately 18.0 miles from the trailhead. There is a sign for the AT showing the distance to Mount Rogers to be 4.5 miles. There is a sign for the Virginia Highlands Trail with distances to Brier Ridge, 2.5 miles and the Crest Trail, 4 miles.

The rugged Cliffside Trail.

Cliffside Trail   2

Length: 2.2 Miles (One Way)
Time: 2 Hours
Elevation Change: 1,500 Feet
Difficulty: Extremely Difficult
USGS Map: Whitetop Mountain
Trailhead: CR 603

How To Get There

Take I-81 to Marion, Va. Take Exit #45 and turn south on US 16. Travel 17.2 miles and turn right on CR 603. Proceed 4.8 miles to parking area on the left. The trailhead is on the left side of the road.

Trail Description

The Cliffside Trail is a very beautiful but very difficult trail. The grade ranges from a low angle walk by streamside greenery to an extremely strenuous and steep climb. There are several ways to access the trail, and many circuit hikes including the Cliffside Trail can be devised. This description will begin from the top of the mountain (as anyone experienced enough, meaning "crazy" enough, to hike it from the bottom up probably doesn't need a description anyway). Although plenty can be said of the difficulty of this trail, it still is highly recommended. If not advanced enough to tackle the beautiful ruggedness of the upper end, please don't forego the section from the Lewis Fork Spur Trail down.

Cliffside Trail begins atop Pine Mountain and can be accessed from the Appalachian Trail or the Lewis Fork Trail. After passing through a gate, the trail will leave the mountain meadow and enter the forest. The gate functions to keep the wild horses that roam the mountain meadow from wandering through the wilderness area. The trail, marked with pink blazes, soon becomes steep and rocky. At about 0.6 miles the trail makes a left turn and the grade becomes more moderate. Shortly after the grade moderates, the Cliffside Trail intersects Lewis Fork Spur Trail (see Lewis Fork Spur Trail description). This trail intersection comes at about 0.75 miles. The Lewis Fork Spur exits to the left and the Old Orchard Trail exits to the right. The Cliffside Trail passes straight through the intersection and continues down the ridge.

After the intersection, Cliffside Trail becomes very steep. The trail is rutted out by runoff. There are more pink blazes, and hemlock grows to the left. Next, the trail grade levels and the forest floor is dominated by mountain laurel. At 1.0 miles the trail approaches the Lewis Fork. There are side trails leading to the creek and possible campsites abound. At 1.25 miles small feeder streams are crossed. There is a campsite at about 1.4 miles. The Cliffside Trail reaches the junction with the Lower Lewis Fork Trail (See Lower Lewis Fork Trail description) at 1.6 miles. The Lower Lewis Fork Trail exits the Cliffside Trail to the right and travels 0.5 miles to the Old Orchard Trail.

Cliffside Trail continues to descend along the creek and passes a weedy meadow. This area looks as though it may have been the sight of a homestead many, many years ago. Several small streams are crossed, and erosion control devices have been placed across the trail. At about 2.1 miles a large wooden bridge is crossed. There is a gate and a Forest Service information center on the far side of the bridge. The trail leaves the forest and enters a meadow. The meadow leads down to CR 603.

Grassy Branch Trail   3

Length: 3.0 miles (One Way)
Time: 1.5 hours
Elevation Change: 520 Feet
Difficulty: Easy
USGS Map: Whitetop Mountain
Trailhead: On CR 603 and CR 600

How To Get There

Take I-81 to Marion, Va. Take Exit #45 and turn south on US 16. Travel 17.2 miles and turn right on CR 603. Proceed 6.9 miles to a small parking area on the right. The trailhead is on the left.

Take I-81 to Marion, Va. Take Exit #45 and turn south on US 16. Travel 17.2 miles and turn right on CR 603. Proceed 9.4 miles and turn left on CR 600. After 100 yards CR 600 turns left again. Proceed 3.9 miles to a parking area on the left. The trailhead is on the left.

Trail Description

The Grassy Branch Trail is a short, easy hike from CR 603 to CR 600. It is located in the southwestern part of the wilderness area. The trail contours the mountainside and crosses many streams, one of which is the Grassy Branch. The hike is about 3 miles long (one way) and can easily be done as an out and back. The forest is thick along the trail and the tree canopy supplies cool shade on even the hottest summer days. There is a small parking spot off of CR 603, but parking is scarce on CR 600. This trail description begins at the parking area on CR 603.

The hike begins near some signs and passes to the right of a small meadow. Within 0.5 miles, the trail approaches a small stream. The trail parallels the stream for a very short distance. Just past the stream, there are a couple of small "trails" to the left. Do not follow these uphill forks, but rather continue to contour and follow the frequent blue blazes. At 0.7 miles, the trail crosses the Grassy Branch and bends right. Over the next mile, there are two more small streams to cross. These are followed by a small wilderness sign and a National Forest property sign.

At 2.0 miles the trail again crosses a creek and bends right. This is the Charlie Branch. The trail crosses two more stream drainages and then bends widely to the right before crossing yet another small creek. Next, the trail follows a couple of switchbacks down the ridge at a low to moderate angle. Shortly after the switches the trail climbs again, finally terminating at CR 600. There is a sign with the following information for the return hike: Charlie Branch 1, Grassy Branch 2, Rt. 603 3.

Helton Creek Trail 4

Lenghth: 3.1 Miles (One Way)
Time: 1.25 Hours
Elevation Change: 720 Feet
Difficulty: Moderate/Difficult
USGS Map: Whitetop Mountain
Trailhead: End of CR 783

How To Get There

Take I-81 to Marion, Va. Take Exit #45 and turn south on US 16. Travel 24.3 miles to US 58 and turn right. Proceed 13.6 miles to CR 783. Turn right and travel 2.0 miles to the end of the road. The road is gravel but is in good shape. The trailhead is located approximately 1.0 miles up the closed road from the parking area.

Trail Description

The Helton Creek Trail starts in farm land pastures, travels along a creek, and then climbs the ridge to join the Virginia Highlands Trail. There is plenty of water available. The Helton Creek Trail can be paired with the Sugar Maple Trail to create a 4.2 mile loop. The Sugar Maple and Helton Creek Trails have the same trailhead.

From the gate the Helton Creek Trail follows a road through pasture land and cowfields. The trail passes through another gate at 0.5 miles. There is a split in the trail at 0.8 miles. To stay on the Helton Creek Trail turn right. Taking a left at this fork leads around the ridge to a junction with the Virginia Highlands Trail near CR 600. Helton Creek Trail turns right and starts up the mountain at a difficult angle. This section of trail consists of right turns steeply climbing the ridge followed by left turns contouring across the ridge. At 1.25 miles the trail crosses a stream, and at 1.5 miles enters the wilderness. There is a wilderness sign at the boundary. The trail crosses a stream. This crossing is quickly followed by two switchbacks. There is a pink blaze on a tree near the right switchback.

At just over two miles, the Helton Creek Trail connects with the Sugar Maple Trail (See Sugar Maple Trail description). To hike the Sugar Maple Trail back to the Helton Creek trailhead, turn right at this junction. To continue along the Helton Creek Trail, make a left at this intersection.

After the intersection with the Sugar Maple Trail, the Helton Creek Trail begins to flatten out. There is a short, steep section within 0.1 miles of the intersection with the Virginia Highlands Trail, and at times the trail can be rocky. The trail continues around the ridge and crosses Helton Creek. In the summer, there are stretches in this section where stinging nettle crowds the trail. This can be particularly bothersome when wearing short pants. At approximately 2.75 miles the Helton Creek Trail joins the Virginia Highlands Trail. There is a sign showing directions to Rhodedendron Gap and Elk Garden.

Lewis Fork Trail   5

Lenght: 2.5 Miles
Time: 1.25 Hours
Elevation Change: 400 Feet
Difficulty: Difficult
USGS Map: Whitetop Mountain
Trailhead: Via Lewis Fork Spur Trail or the Cliffside Trail

How To Get There

Via the Lewis Fork Spur Trail or the Cliffside Trail

Trail Description

The Lewis Fork Trail is a rocky climb to the top of Pine Mountain. The hike begins moderately but becomes more difficult near the top. Beginning at an intersection about 2.1 miles from the Mount Rogers Trail, the Lewis Fork travels along the ridge side. Be aware that the Lewis Fork Trail is very rocky and, when it rains, very muddy. The hike can become difficult and disheartening. However, for those who like a more rugged hike, the Lewis Fork Trail may be the answer. The high meadow that greets one at the top of the mountain is surely worth the effort. To avoid the rocks and mud nearer the top, the Lewis Fork Spur Trail can be utilized. The Lewis Fork Spur Trail drops off at one point and, coupled with Cliffside and CR 603, can make a long but pleasant circuit.

Wild horses on Pine Mountain.

To hike the Lewis Fork Trail, follow the trail description for Mount Rogers Trail to the intersection with the Lewis Fork Spur Trail. The trail exits this intersection to the left and narrows substantially. Blue blazes mark the trail. The grade descends slightly and then becomes very steep. The grade levels off and there are many blazes. The intersection with the Lewis Fork Spur Trail is reached and there is a sign (See Lewis Fork Spur Trail description). The Lewis Fork Trail exits to the right as the hike resumes its up-slope direction. The Lewis Fork Spur Trail descends to the left.

The next two miles of trail are easy to follow but difficult to hike. The trail is often muddy and rocks are frequent. Be very careful about footing to prevent ankle injury. One interesting landmark comes at 0.7 miles as a small stream passes under the trail. The gurgling of the stream can be heard but the trail is on dry dirt. There are tall, straight tulip poplar and mountain laurel throughout this area. The trail becomes a series of long upward sections followed by short descents. The overall trend is a gain in elevation. The trail is rocky and one can expect mud between the rocks.

At 2.25 miles the trail passes through a livestock gate and enters a turn around spot for horseback riders. The undergrowth is composed mainly of tall grass indicating that the high meadow is near. The intersection with Cliffside Trail is reached at 2.5 miles. A right on the Cliffside Trail leads to the top of Pine Mountain, while a left leads back to CR 603.

Lewis Fork Spur Trail   6

Length: 0.8 Miles (One Way)
Time: 30 minutes
Elevation Change: 360 Feet
Difficulty: Easy
USGS Map: Whitetop Mountain
Trailhead: Mount Rogers Trail

How To Get There

Via the Mount Rogers Trail and the Cliffside Trail

Trail Description

The Lewis Fork Spur is a trail that branches off of the Lewis Fork Trail. The Spur contours through the Lewis Fork drainage at a lower elevation than the Lewis Fork Trail. The Spur also intersects with Cliffside Trail and Old Orchard Trail. Lewis Fork Spur is short, easy, and pleasant. Combined with neighboring trails, the Lewis Fork Spur can be used in various circuit hikes.

To get to the Lewis Fork Spur, follow the Mount Rogers Trail to the intersection with the Lewis Fork Trail. Take a left at this intersection and follow the Lewis Fork Trail about 0.5 miles to the intersection with the Lewis Fork Spur Trail. There is a sign at this intersection and the Spur Trail drops down to the left. The trail is wide and blazed blue; it is very easy to follow. At about 0.3 miles it crosses a stream. There is a small log bridge over the stream. The next section of trail can be muddy during rainy months. The Lewis Fork is reached at 0.6 miles. The angle of the trail is moderate and there is a campsite to the left. As the stream drops off to the left there is another potentially muddy section of trail. The trail crosses another small stream. There are rocks set up accross the stream to control erosion. Just beyond the stream, the Spur Trail joins the Cliffside and Old Orchard Trails.

From this point the Cliffside Trail or Old Orchard Trail can be hiked down to CR 603, leaving a walk along the road back to the Mount Rogers trailhead. Hiking up the Cliffside is definitely not recommended, but experienced hikers could use it along with the upper Lewis Fork Trail to create a circuit. Just remember, hiking up Cliffside Trail is strenuous and tiring; allow for extra time, food, and water (See Cliffside Trail description).

Lower Lewis Fork Trail   7

Lenght: 0.6 Miles
Time: 20 Minutes
Elevation Change: 100 Feet
Difficulty: Easy
USGS Map: Whitetop
Trailhead: Old Orchard Trail and the Cliffside Trail

<u>How To Get There</u>

Via the Old Orchard Trail or the Cliffside Trail

<u>Trail Description</u>

The Lower Lewis Fork Trail is a connecter between Old Orchard and Cliffside Trails. The trail is easy to hike and is visually rewarding. Coupled with the aforementioned trails, these three trails make a very pleasant circuit hike. The trail is marked with blue blazes.

The trail exits the Old Orchard Trail to the left and descends slightly. While descending, there is a hemlock grove on the right, and a large boulder to the left. At about 0.3 miles there is a large area of running cedar covering the ground. At 0.5 miles there is a blaze on the left. The intersection with the Cliffside Trail comes at 0.6 miles. A right takes the hiker to CR 603.

Mount Rogers Trail   8

Length: 6.4 Miles (One Way)
Time: 3.5 Hours
Elevation Change: 2,000 Feet
Difficulty: Moderate/Difficult
USGS Map: Whitetop Mountain
Trailhead: CR 603

<u>How To Get There</u>

Take I-81 to Marion, Va. Take Exit #45 and turn south on US 16. Travel 17.2 miles and turn right on CR 603. Proceed 5.7 miles to a parking area on the right. The trailhead is located on the left side of the road.

Trail Description

The Mount Rogers Trail is a "must hike" because it travels to the summit of the tallest mountain in Virginia. Any self respecting Virginia hiker must do this trail at some point. The walk is steep at times but overall not too bad. From bottom to top expect about 5.9 miles of hiking. This makes for a long trip if one expects to hike it in one day. A better idea is to take a backpack and connect the Mount Rogers Trail with a few other trails in the wilderness area. There is one important note: There is no view from the summit of Mount Rogers. There are, however, excellent views from the high mountain pasture on the southeastern side of Mount Rogers. Another good reason to make the hike is to see the Fraser fir and red spruce forest which occupies the summit. The summit of Mount Rogers is a popular area, and the Mount Rogers Trail is one of the few wilderness hikes during which you should expect to see several hikers. Water is scarce along this trail so be sure to carry enough for a long day.

The hike begins from the parking lot on CR 603. The trailhead is on the opposite side of the road. The trail will be obvious as there is a sign and a boardwalk leading into the woods. A wildernes sign is passed within 0.25 miles. The trail is blazed blue and is easy to follow. Immediately, the trail begins to climb and there are several switchbacks. There are railroad tie bridges crossing creeks between switchsbacks. At about 2.5 miles there is a pleasant camping area (no water) and a sign. The Lewis Fork Spur Trail (See Lewis Fork Spur Trail description) branches off to the left.

The trail leaves this area and continues to gain elevation through hardwood forest. At about 3.0 miles the area becomes damp and hemlock trees dot the landscape. Just beyond this damp area, the trail grade is moderate. There is a steady gain in elevation. The trail in this area wraps around the western side of the mountain. At 4.8 miles the trail links up with the AT (See AT description). To reach the summit, turn left on the AT and continue climbing until reaching the Mount Rogers Summit Trail. An interesting side note: At the intersection of the Mount Rogers Trail and the AT, the Tennessee Valley Divide is crossed. The Tennessee Valley Divde is the break in the drainage basins between the Atlantic Ocean and the Mississippi River; water on one side flows to the Atlantic while water on the other flows to the Mississippi.

Upon reaching the AT turn left. The blazes change to white. There are a couple of switchbacks interspersed with the contouring of the mountainside. An "S" curve is followed by a descent to the

An incoming storm

high mountain meadow which covers the south side of Mt. Rogers. There is a fence and boulders are visable to the southwest. The Virginia Highland Trail passes by these boulders. At the fence the AT makes a left turn and continues to contour the mountainside.

The AT passes by a campsite, large red spruce, and a several small streams. The trail can be wet in this area at anytime of the year. Next, the AT enters the meadow and starts up again. After about five minutes in the meadow, the Mount Rogers Summit Trail exits the AT to the left. The trail is about 5.8 miles from the trailhead. In the meadow are many mountain ash; these trees produce an abundance of red berries in the fall. Turn left onto the Mount Rogers Summit Trail. The trail grade becomes steeper and the blazes change back to blue. At about 6.0 miles the Summit Trail reenters the forest. The forest at 5,600 feet is markedly different than what was seen at 3,800 feet. Here, there are red spruce and Frazier fir,trees which established themselves in Virginia during the last ice age. In todays Virginia, their only habitat is the high elevations. There is an understory of moss and fern that gives a distinct western mountain feel. The summit is reached and is marked by a small sign. There are medium-sized boulders to sit and rest on.

From the summit there are a few options regarding the return. Many trails connect with the AT and attempts to list them all would be futile. If one is limited to a day, hike the best option is to backtrack. If you have extra time ponder the map and do some exploring. The area is expansive and many days can be spent near the summit of Virginia.

Old Orchard Trail   9

Length: 1.3 Miles (One Way)
Time: 30 Minutes
Elevation Change: 440 Feet
Difficulty: Easy
USGS Map: Whitetop Mountain
Trailhead: CR 603

<u>How To Get There</u>

Take I-81 to Marion, Va. Take Exit #45 and turn south US 16. Travel 17.2 miles and turn right on CR 603. Proceed 4.5 miles to a small trailhead on the left. Parking can be found about 0.3 miles up the road.

<u>Trail Description</u>

Old Orchard Trail takes the hiker into the wilderness and is useful for accessing other trails. Old Orchard Trail crosses the AT twice and also provides easy access to the Lewis Fork Trail. The trail is very pleasant and easy to hike. When coupled with the Lewis Fork and Cliffside Trail, these three trails create an enjoyable circuit hike. There are no blazes on Old Orchard Trail, but it is easy to follow.

The trail begins at a very small parking area off of CR 603. There is a sign stating that the Orchard Spur Trail is 1 mile away and that the Lewis Fork Trail is 1.5 miles away. Near the beginning is a barrier and the trail is covered with gravel. After a short distance there is a left bend and the trail starts an easy climb. A right turn at approximately 0.2 miles is followed by a wilderness sign at 0.25 miles. The trail passes over a drainage pipe and at 0.5 miles crosses the AT for the first time just before bending to the right.

At about 0.75 miles, after passing a boulder, the grade becomes moderate. The Orchard Spur Trail is crossed at the 0.9 miles. Old Orchard Trail makes a right and the moderate angle continues. After a wet runoff area, the Old Orchard Trail crosses the AT again. Old Orchard Trail curves right and begins contouring the side of the ridge. The grade is easy through this section. A small meadow with some apple trees is passed at about 1.1 miles. In this meadow is the Old

Orchard Trail Shelter. The orchard contains small apple trees and the overstory is composed mainly of maple. This is a very interesting section of the wilderness and is highly recommended.

After passing the meadow, the grade of the trail changes and begins an easy descent. At 1.3 miles the Old Orchard Trail intersects with the Lewis Fork Trail. There is a sign at this intersection. The Lewis Fork Trail continues up the mountain, crossing Cliffside Trail and ultimately leading to the Mount Rogers Trail.

Sugar Maple Trail   10

Length: 2.5 Miles
Time: 1 Hour
Elevation Change: 660 Feet
Difficulty: Moderate
USGS Map: Whitetop Mountain
Trailhead: CR 783

How To Get There

Take I-81 to Marion, Va. Take Exit #45 and turn south on US 16. Travel 24.3 miles to US 58 and turn right. Proceed 13.6 miles to CR 783. Turn right and travel 2.0 miles to the end of the road. The road is gravel but is in good shape.

Trail Description

The Sugar Maple Trail is an excellent path into the Lewis Fork Wilderness; a path that is less frequented by the summit and AT hikers. The Sugar Maple Trail is relatively short and can be used in combination with the Helton Creek Trail to make an excellent circuit. Water is relatively scarce except at the very beginning of the hike.

The walk begins at the end of CR 783. The road continues through cow fields and a sign points out the directions to both the Helton Creek Trail and Sugar Maple Trail. The Sugar Maple Trail exits to the right and slowly starts up the mountain. The first section of the trail continues through the pastures. After about five minutes of walking the trail reaches a forested drainage basin. In this basin there is a right switchback and the trail continues up the ridge. After passing through a gate, the meadow briefly opens up again. The grade is moderate.

An old homestead on the Helton Creek Trail.

After crossing the meadow the trail narrows. At about 0.75 miles the Sugar Maple Trail enters the wilderness. A boundary sign is passed. Just beyond the sign, the trail makes a left switchback followed by a right and then another left. The area surrounding these switchbacks can be very wet and muddy. After another right and left switchback, the trail levels out. These last couple of switchbacks are connected by moderate grades.

After the switchbacks, the trail levels and begins a slight descent. This continues about 0.6 miles until an "S" turn brings the Sugar Maple Trail to an end at the Helton Creek Trail intersection. A right at this intersection leads to the Virginia Highlands Trail and AT. A left leads down the mountain on the Helton Creek Trail and actually goes back to the starting point on CR 783.

Virginia Highlands Trail   11

Length: 3.0 Miles
Time: 1.5 Hours
Elevation Change: 640 Feet
Difficulty: Moderate
USGS Map: Whitetop Mountain
Trailhead: CR 600 and Grayson Highlands State Park

How To Get There

Take I-81 to Marion, Va. Take Exit #45 and turn south on US 16. Travel 17.2 miles and turn right on CR 603. Proceed 9.4 miles and turn left on CR 600. After 100 yards CR 600 turns left again. Travel 5.3 miles to the top of the mountain. Parking is on the right.

The other access is at Massies Gap in the Grayson Highlands State Park. The park is located just off US 58 about 7.6 miles west from the intersections of US 16 and US 58. At the park entrance, turn right and follow the signs to Massie's Gap.

Trail Description

The Virginia Highlands Trail is a long, wide, muddy horse trail. The blazes for the trail are orange. It is not a very pleasant hike, and thus is not recommended except for use in connecting with other trails. There are many hoof prints and manure is a frequent sight (and smell). The entire length of tha Virginia Highlands Trail through the wilderness is about 3.0 miles. There is camping in the high meadow area, however water is scarce.

From CR 600 it is almost 2 miles to the intersection with the Helton Creek Trail (See Helton Creek Trail description), which exits right. Prior to reaching the Helton Creek Trail, the trail passes through beautiful mountain meadows. About 0.75 miles from the Helton Creek Trail junction, The Virginia Highlands Trail enters Deep Gap. The AT also crosses this gap. There is a sign stating that camping is no longer permitted in the area because of overuse.

After climbing through a small gap on Brier Ridge, the Virginia Highlands Trail exits the wilderness. It continues to parallel the wilderness until reaching the Thomas Knob Trail Shelter. At the shelter, the trail turns east and heads toward Grayson Highlands State Park.

Little Dry Run Wilderness

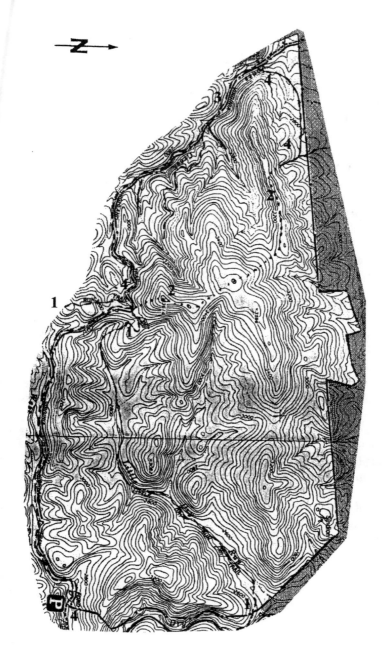

Little Dry Run

The Little Dry Run Wilderness is located in the southwestern corner of Wythe County. This small wilderness, approximately 3,400 acres, is about thirteen miles southwest of Wytheville, Virginia. It is in the Mt. Rogers District of the Jefferson National Forest. Little Dry Run was created by Congress in 1984.

The wilderness encompasses a large shoulder on the northern side of Iron Mountain. Jones Creek and West Branch form the southern boundary, and US 16 forms the eastern boundary. Little Dry Run, from which the wilderness gets its name, is the main drainage source for the interior of the wilderness. Little Dry Run tumbles and crashes in a northwestern direction from its source between Iron Mountain and Little Dry Run Wilderness.

Little Dry Run Wilderness is a rugged area with few trails. The Little Dry Run Wilderness has only one maintained trail within the wilderness itself. This is the Little Dry Run Trail. The Virginia Highlands Trail borders the wilderness area to the south, but does not enter Little Dry Run Wilderness. There is plenty of water along these trails, but it is best to treat the water before drinking. Bushwhacking is the only other avenue for exploring some of the more remote regions. However, it can be difficult as the terrain is steep, water is scarce, and the mountain laurel is thick.

The forest of the Little Dry Run is primarily oak-hickory forest common to the eastern United States. However, in the sheltered coves are many large cove hardwoods as well as hemlock and white pine.

Areas of interest in the wilderness are limited. There is a scenic view of the Dry Run Valley from the Virginia Highlands Trail. and the Little Dry Run Trail is a beautiful hike any time of year. Finally, Comers Rock while not in the wilderness area itself provides a fine view to the north and east. Comers Rock is a large rock outcrop located near the southern end of the Little Dry Run Trail.

Finally, be aware that hunters use the area during hunting season. Therefore, try to avoid hiking during this time.

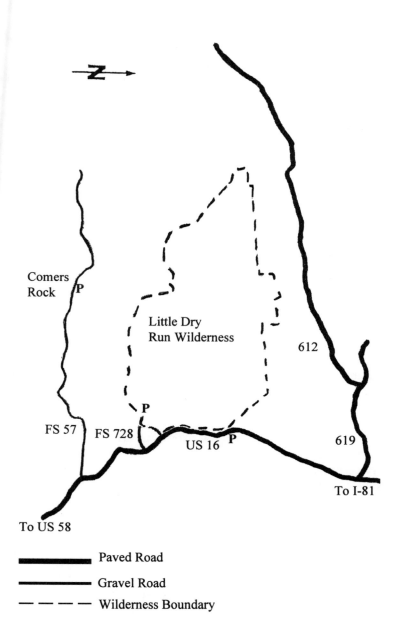

Little Dry Run 1

Length: 3.9 Miles (One Way)
Time: 1.5 Hours
Elevation Change: 1,120 Feet
Difficulty: Moderate
USGS Map: Speedwell
Trailhead: US 21 and FS 57

How To Get There

To reach the parking area at Comers Rock, take I-81 to Exit #70. Turn south on US 21 and travel 17.9 miles. Turn right on FS 57 and proceed 2 miles to the Comers Rock Campground. To reach the lower parking area, take I-81 to Exit #70. Turn south on US 21 and travel 15.6 miles. There is a parking area on the left, The trailhead is on the right side of the just south of the parking area.

Trail Description

Starting at 3,740 feet by the Comers Rock Campground, the Little Dry Run Trail is a pleasant walk down the ridge. As the name suggests, the majority of the walk involves following Little Dry Run from its origin high atop Iron Mountain to where it exits the wilderness. The trail is easy to hike when started at the top of the mountain and there is ample water for filtering. Portions of the trail can be difficult to follow, but if you stay with the stream the trail reappears.

The trail begins at northwestern end of the Comers Rock campground, named after Comers Rock which lies farther up the mountain. This rocky point can be accessed by either driving up the mountain past the campground or via a branch off of the Little Dry Run Trail. From the northwestern end of the campground, the Little Dry Run Trail is marked by a sign which reads Iron Mountain Trail. Follow the trail to another sign which shows the hiker that Comers Rock and Hale Lake lie to the left and that the West Fork of Dry Run is one mile to the right. To state the obvious - make a right to follow the Little Dry Run Trail.

Shortly after this second sign the trail takes a left and starts down the mountain. At about 0.25 miles the trail bends to the right through what is the beginnings of the Run. The descent is moderate. The trail makes another right and travels more directly down the ridge. The forest is mostly young hardwoods such as oak and hickory with

Bloodroot, a plant in the Poppy family.

a few scattered pines. At about 0.5 miles there are several bends through downed timber. There are steep sections of varying degrees of difficulty. The trail begins to contour the mountain after 0.75 miles of hiking. After the path crosses the top of the finger ridge, there will be a descent of 0.5 miles to the intersection with the Virginia Highlands Trail. The Virginia Highlands Trail is 1.25 miles from the trailhead.

The Little Dry Run Trail crosses the Virginia Highlands Trail, and there is a register for the hiker to sign. The Virginia Highlands Trail travels east-west and forms the southern boundary of the wilderness area (See Virginia Highlands Trail description). From the register the trail becomes rugged and difficult to follow. The walk is challenging and rewarding. For most of the next section the trail is intimately acquainted with the Dry Run (stream). Therefore, if you wander off the trail, follow the stream down the mountain and then look for the trail again.

From the register the walk begins at a mild angle. However, within two minutes the trail turns right and down a portion of fist sized rocks. There are yellow blazes so be on the lookout. Follow the blazes and the rocks. The trail bends left and levels out. The stream is on the right. The forest is interesting with hemlock forming the canopy, rhodendrondon in the understory, and teaberry covering the ground. At approximately 0.5 miles from the register the trail crosses the stream twice. There is a significant amount of downed timber, and the trail becomes more difficult to follow. Look for

101

yellow blazes on the trees and footprints in the mud; these indicators serve as a guide for following the trail. If you are in doubt stay on the left side of the stream. This area sounds more dificult than it really is, but its not as obvious as following the AT.

At a little over 1.0 miles from the register, the path opens up and becomes more discernable. Dry Run is crossed several times and there are many large hemlock. The trail follows the stream for approximately another mile. There is an intersection at about 2.5 miles from the register. The Little Dry Run Trail branches right, while hiking straight leads to private property. Take a right at the intersection, then a left after about fifty yards. The trail climbs uphill then begins to contour the mountainside as it wraps around the ridge. After passing a wilderness boundary sign, the trail starts to descend and US 21 is visible to the left. There is a left switchback. The stream is crossed and the trail leads the hiker to a register and the road. Across the road there is a parking lot and a Forest Service information center. Although the walk up the mountain from this parking area is a nice one, due to the difficulty in following the trail it is recommended to hike the Little Dry Run from top to bottom (as described here).

Ridge Top Area Bushwhack   2

Length: Varies
Time: Varies
Difficulty: Difficult
Elevation Change: Varies
USGS Maps: Speedwell
Trailhead: See How To Get There

How To Get There

One way to access the ridge top is to walk to the junction of the Little Dry Run Trail and the Virginia Highlands Trail. From this junction hike north and uphill. Another route is to follow the Virginia Highlands Extension to the fork, take the right fork and follow it to the top.

Trail Description

There is no trail along the ridge top. However, the ridge area does have nice views to the north and south. The high area around the junction of the two trails presents some fairly open hiking and leads to the highest point in the wilderness area at 3,614 feet. There is a clearing and some turkey blinds are in the area.

The northern and southern ends of the ridge are very similar. Both are very narrow and forested by small hardwoods and pine. There is also a great deal of laurel and brier on the ridges. The area is very dry so pack plenty to drink. Finally, because of the difficult nature of this ridge, carry a good map and compass.

Virginia Highlands Trail   3

Length: 4.8 Miles (One Way)
Time: 2 Hours
Difficulty: Moderate
Elevation Change: 800 Feet
USGS Maps: Speedwell
Trailhead: FS 728

How To Get There

Take I-81 to Exit #70 and US 21. Turn south on US 21 and travel 16.8 miles. Turn right on FS 748 and proceed 0.6 miles to a parking area. There is a picnic table in the parking area. One note of caution, there is a shallow ford prior to reaching the parking area.

Trail Description

The Virginia Highlands Trail is a horse trail which stretches across much of the highlands of Southwestern Virginia. This particular section of the trail forms the southern boundary of the Little Dry Run Wilderness Area. The trail is well maintained and is more like a road than a trail.

From the parking area, the road climbs gradually. The West Fork flows along the left side of the trail. There is a barrier of posts about 100 yards beyond the parking area. The creek bottom is full of old hemlock, white pine, and large cove hardwoods. Rhododendron completes the understory. At 0.4 miles the trail crosses the creek via a culvert which provides a makeshift bridge.

There are several small clearings left of the trail. The right side of the trail is composed of hardwoods such as hickory, oak, and maple. There is a great deal of storm damage. Once past the clearings, a road exits left. This road is 2.1 miles from the trailhead. To continue on the Virginia Highlands Trail bear right.

A scene from the Virginia Highlands Trail.

The climb becomes moderate as it leads to a clearing. There is a scenic view of the Little Dry Run Valley. The climb becomes easier and soon a gap between two high points is reached. In this gap, the Virginia Highlands Trail intersects the Little Dry Run Trail (See Little Dry Run Trail description). There is a Little Dry Run Wilderness sign and a trail register. The junction of the Virginia Highlands Trail with the Little Dry Run Trail is 2.6 miles from the parking area.

Beyond this intersection, the trail descends at a moderate pace. The forest is composed of medium sized hardwoods such as red oak and hickory. The trail follows Jones Creek down the mountain to a small clearing and a flat area.

At 3.8 miles, in this flat area, there is a small trail exiting right which leads to a small clearing and then to another, larger clearing. This is an excellent place to camp. This short trail continues for another 0.4 miles before ending.

The Virginia Highlands Trail is the left fork at the intersection with the small trail. The Virginia Highlands continues downhill past some posts, crosses the Jones Creek, and enters an area of tall hemlock. The creek is crossed again and there is a trail/road to the right which leads to a dead end after about 0.75 miles. The Virginia Highlands Trail again crosses the creek and another intersection is reached. The road on the right leads a short distance up the mountainside before it ends. This road is about 4.3 miles from the trailhead. The

Virginia Highlands Trail is the the left fork at this intersection.

The trail crosses the creek before a switchback back to the left and begins to climb. The creek crossing is not difficult. At the switchback, the Virginia Highlands Trail leaves the Little Dry Run Wilderness behind. There is a trail which continues along the creek (See Virginia Highlands Extension description).

Virginia Highlands Extension   4

Length: 1.3 Miles (One Way)
Time: 45 MInutes
Difficulty: Easy
Elevation Change: 550 Feet
USGS Maps: Speedwell
Trailhead: Reached Via the Viginia Highlands Trail

How To Get There

This trail is accessed via the Virginia Highlands Trail and is not located on any maps. See the trail description for the Virginia Highlands Trail for the easiest access to this trail.

Trail Description

This trail is a short "out and back" along the northern side of the wilderness. The trail is well maintained and appears to be used primarily by horseback riders interested in accessing the Virginia Highlands Trail. The trail also provides access to the ridge top.

This trail leaves the Virginia Highlands Trail and continues to follow Jones Creek and eventually leads to private property. The distance from the HighlandsTrail to private property is about 0.25 miles. Near the boundary line, the trail crosses Jones Creek and begins to climb. There is a field to the right. The forest to the left is composed of small pine and laurel. The trail climbs at a moderate grade. A short trail to the left leads to private property and a large field. There is a right bend and then a left bend.

After the bends, the trail becomes slightly steeper but still not difficult. The trail forks. The left fork leads downhill, out of the wilderness and onto private land. The right fork leads up the mountain, almost reaching the top. The road up the mounain ends on a shoulder and the bushwhack to the top is not difficult.

Little
Wilson
Creek
Wilderness

Little Wilson Creek

Little Wilson Creek Wilderness, located approximately eleven miles south of Marion, Virginia is a small primitive area encompassing approximately 3,900 acres. The wilderness is located in the western end of Grayson County, in the Mt. Rogers District of the Jefferson National Forest. This upland area was included in the National Wilderness Preservation System in 1984.

Little Wilson Creek occupies the southeastern portion of Pine Mountain and includes three peaks over 4,000 feet. The wilderness gets its name from Little Wilson Creek, a small creek draining the central portion of the wilderness area. Many small springs feed this creek. Little Wilson Creek drains into Wilson Creek. Wilson Creek forms the southwestern boundary of the wilderness area.

The trail system in the wilderness is extensive. There are approximately twenty-five miles of trail in the area and along its perimeter. All of the trails are well marked and easy to follow. Most of the trails are in excellent condition and the hiking is easy. Many of the trails are open to both foot and horse travel. The trails seem to be used frequently, but are not overcrowded. The Hightree Rock Trail is probably the least used trail in the wilderness area. If solitude is the goal, this is the trail to hike

There are both forested regions and grassy balds within the wilderness. One large bald borders the wilderness and is reached via the Bearpen Trail. The forest of Little Wilson Creek is very impressive. It consists primarily of oak, hickory, and maple. In some of the wetter areas, large Frazier magnolia and yellow birch can be found. Finally, in the higher elevations of the wilderness red spruce and Frazier fir thrive.

Areas of interest in the wilderness include a beautiful, boulder strewn meadow on the Bearpen Trail. The First Peak Trail offers many panoramic views. The Little Wilson Creek Trail is also a beautiful trail. This trail parallels Little Wilson Creek as it tumbles to Wilson Creek.

Finally, be aware that the Mount Rogers area and Pine Mountain in specific are major deer hunting areas. There are many hunters in the area during hunting season. Also, because of the high altitude of the Mount Rogers area weather can change quickly. When packing for the hike, be prepared for severe weather. It is better to carry warm clothes and not need them, than to wish you had them if the weather should turns cold.

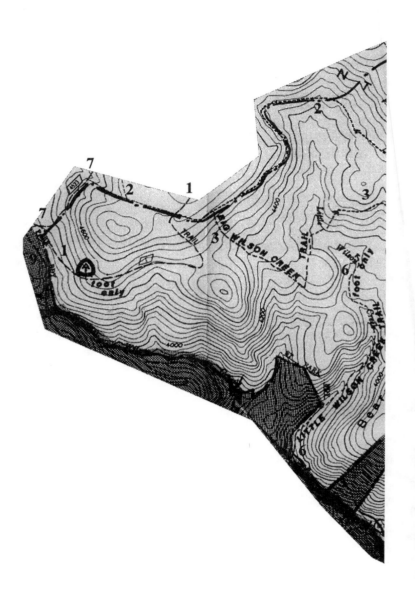

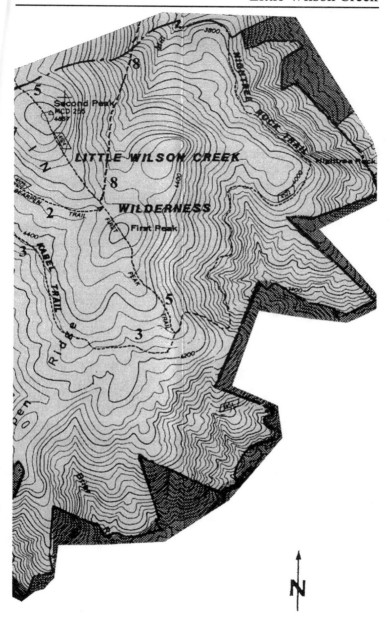

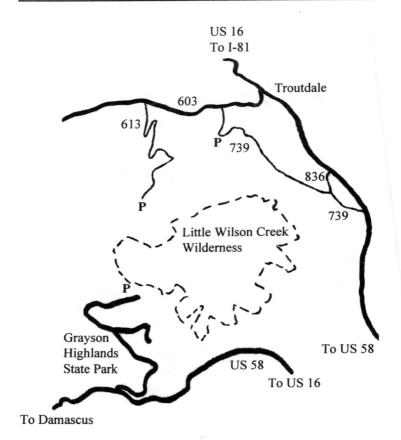

Appalachian Trail   1

Length: 1.3 Miles
Time: 45 Minutes
Difficulty: Easy
Elevation Change: 400 Feet
USGS Maps: Troutdale
Trailhead: Scales Trail or Bearpen Trail

How To Get There

Travel to Grayson Highlands State Park. The park is located just off US 58 about 7.6 miles west from the intersections of US 16 and US 58. At the park entrance, turn right and follow the signs to the campground area. There is a sign for the Wilson Creek Trail. The parking area is on the left near the campground store.

Trail Description

For a complete description of the AT through the Little Wilson Creek Wilderness, please refer to the AT description in Lewis Fork Wilderness.

Bearpen Trail   2

Length: 2.8 Miles
Time: 1.5 Hours
Difficulty: Easy
Elevation Change: 250 Feet
USGS Maps: Troutdale
Trailhead: Via Scales Trail or First Peak Trail

How To Get There

Travel to Grayson Highlands State Park. The park is located just off US 58 about 7.6 miles west from the intersections of US 16 and US 58. At the park entrance, turn right and follow the signs to the campground area. There is a sign for the Wilson Creek Trail.

Trail Description

The Bearpen Trail is a horse trail which passes along the northern boundary of the wilderness and then turns toward the center of the Little Wilson Creek Wilderness Area. The trail does not have a trailhead that can be reached by vehicle; therefore, hiking is required to reach the Bearpen Trail. The trail, marked with orange blazes, contours along the side of Pine Mountain and connects the Scales Trail with the First Peak Trail. The trail features both great forests and huge meadows. One major drawback is the mud created by horses. This problem exists year-round.

The trail is best accessed from Grayson Highlands State Park. Hike up the Wilson Creek Trail to the Scales Trail. The Bearpen Trail intersects the Scales Trail. There is a small spring near the beginning of Bearpen Trail. Shortly after this spring, the trail climbs to a big grassy bald. There are many large rocks in this bald. Hike through the bald and begin a gradual descent to the woods.

Just after entering the woods, there is a gate. On the other side of the gate is a small wilderness sign, and just beyond this sign is the junction with the AT. A sign at the junction gives the distance to the First Peak Trail (2.0 miles). The trail continues in a series of easy ups and downs, and the woods are beautiful.

After 1.25 miles, the Big Wilson Creek Trail (See Big Wilson Creek Trail description) exits the Bearpen Trail to the right. The grade is easy at the trail junction. After the junction with the Big Wilson Creek Trail, several small springs bubble out of the ground and form small creeks. These creeks cross the path and the trail becomes very muddy. The springs also provide enough moisture for yellow birch to thrive. The trail passes through another gate and begins a gradual uphill climb. The trail continues to be muddy. There is a small wilderness sign near the gate.

There is a small clearing at the end of the trail. A sign gives directions for the Bearpen Trail and the First Peak Trail.

Big Wilson Creek/Kabel Trails   3

Length: 2.7 miles (One Way)
Time: 1.5 Hours
Elevation Change: 440 Feet
Difficulty: Easy/Moderate
USGS Map: Troutdale
Trailhead: Via the Bearpen Trail or First Peak Trail

The Big Wilson Creek

How To Get There

Via the Bearpen Trail and The First Peak Trail

Trail Description

The Big Wilson and Kabel Trails are two of the few trails that lie completely within a wilderness and are accessible solely via another trail. Big Wilson connects the Bearpen with Kabel Trail. Kabel Trail is an extension of the Big Wilson Trail and leads to the intersection with First Peak and Hightree Rock Trails. First Peak trail is a "must hike" that passes over the summits of three separate four-thousand foot peaks.

From the Bearpen Trail, at a marked junction, the Big Wilson Trail exits to the southeast at a sign. If coming from the AT, the Big Wilson will be a right turn. The trail descends for nearly a mile until it intersects with Kaleb Trail. The grade to this junction is steep at times. Be on the lookout for a Kaleb Trail sign on the left. The Kaleb Trail makes a sharp left. Most maps show the Kaleb Trail starting at the drainage area to the east. It does not matter what you call it, just remember to take the left at this sign. From this intersection it looks as though Big Wilson may continue down the ridge. It does for a short distance but then runs out, and the hike back up the ridge to the Kaleb Trail is steep and unpleasant.

From the sign, Kaleb Trail contours with only slight changes in trail elevation. The trail comes to a stream and meadow at approximately 0.5 miles. To access the Little Wilson Creek Trail (See Little Wilson Creek Trail description) bushwhack down this stream until the trail is reached (stay on the left side of the stream). Continuing on the Kaleb Trail, there is a short, steep incline following the meadow. The climb ends when the trail makes a right turn onto what looks like a separate trail. This is still the Kaleb Trail. When traveling back in the opposite direction on the Kaleb Trail, be on the lookout because the trail dives over the ridge. It is easy to miss this turn and continue to contour the ridge.

After the steep section, the Kaleb Trail makes a slow, easy trek around the ridge to the intersection with First Peak and Hightree Rock Trails. Kaleb travels over several drainage streams. Some crossings are raised footpaths that avoid mud, and some are not. The area is damp and green plants cover the ground, though, there is little water available for filtration. Continuing along the trail there are some very old fence posts to the right. Shortly after the fence posts the trail turns left and starts uphill again. After an easy climb, the trail reaches the junction with First Peak and Hightree Rock Trails. This trail junction is obvious.

Hightree Rock Trail   4

Length: 3.3 Miles
Time: 1.5 Hours
Difficulty: Moderate
Elevation Change: 520 Feet
USGS Maps: Troutdale
Trailhead: Via the Kabel Trail or The First Peak Trail

How To Get There

Via the Kabel Trail of the First Peak Trail

Trail Description

The Hightree Rock Trail is best accessed from within the wilderness at its junction with the Kabel Trail and the First Peak Trail. The Hightree Rock Trail winds across the eastern end of the Little Dry Run Wilderness exiting on CR 739. However, shortly after exiting the wilderness, the trail enters private property and the land owners do not like trespassers. The trail, marked with orange blazes, passes through stands of large timber as well as areas of small pine and gnarled chestnut oak. There is an excellent view at the small rock outcrop called Hightree Rocks.

This trail description begins at the Hightree Rock Trail junction with the Kabel Trail and the First Peak Trail. The area around this junction is very flat and there are several nice campsites. After about 0.4 miles, the trail descends at a moderate rate with a left switchback. There are many large oaks in this area. There is a right switchback, and then, just before a left switchback there is a huge bent oak.

The area beyond these switchbacks is fairly flat and there are several campsites. The trail intersects with an old road, and there is a great deal of brush indicating little use. The path enters a large bowl, and there are three small springs at the end of the bowl. This area is about 1.3 miles from the junction.

On he opposite side of the bowl the land is very dry. Mountain laurel, chestnut oak, and small Virginia pine dominate the landscape. The trail climbs over the shoulder of the mountain and the large hardwoods signal more moist conditions.. There is a left bend and the trail drops rapidly. There is a good view to the east. On the right there is a small sign for Hightree Rock and about 75 feet to the right is a rock outcrop with an excellent view to the east. Hightree Rock is approximately 2.0 miles from the First Peak Trail junction. At this point the best option is to return to this junction. The trail, however, does continue.

The trail begins a long gradual descent. Two springs are crossed and some large boulders are visible to the left. A small wilderness sign is passed, and the trail takes on the characteristics of a road. At a bend in the road, there is a small creek and an old cabin. This cabin is 3.2 miles from the junction. This is where private property begins. This road eventually ends at CR 739, about 5.3 miles from the trailhead.

First Peak Trail 5

Length: 3.2 Miles
Time: 1.5 Hours
Difficulty: Moderate
Elevation Change: 530 Feet
USGS Maps: Troutdale
Trailheads: CR 613 and Grayson Highlands State Park

How To Get There

Travel to Grayson Highlands State Park. The park is located just off US 58, 7.6 miles west from the intersections of US 16 and US 58. At the park entrance, turn right and follow the signs to the campground area. There is a sign for the Wilson Creek Trail. The parking area is on the left near the campground store.

Take I-81 to Marion, Va. Take Exit #45 and turn south on US 16. Travel 17.2 miles and turn right on CR 603. Proceed 2.8 miles to CR 613 and turn left. Travel 3.7 miles to the Scales area. CR 613 is a rough road and not recommended for passenger cars.

Mountain laurel blooms in early June.

Trail Description

The First Peak Trail crosses over three high summits on Pine Mountain in the Little Wilson Wilderness. The trail has many great views of the surrounding mountains and lowlands. The First Peak Trail wanders through high meadows and wooded areas.

The trailhead is located at the end of FS 613 at an area known as Scales. Near a confusing intersection of trails, the First Peak Trail proceeds in a southeasterly direction. The trail begins an easy climb to a high shoulder on Pine Mountain. There are many views in this upland meadow.

The trail is generally flat but begins a slight descent to a saddle. Just before reaching the saddle and at 0.9 miles, Third Peak Trail exits to the left. Not far beyond this junction, the trail passes through a gate into a nice wooded area. Blueberries and table mountain pine can be found in the saddle.

The climb up Third Peak begins. The climb is not difficult. The trail does not pass directly over the top but skirts to the right. The area near the crest is reached at 1.3 miles. The trail begins to descend to the saddle between Third Peak and Second Peak. This descent is moderate and short. In the saddle lies the boundary of the Little Wilson Creek Wilderness. The climb to the top of Second Peak is a short, moderate climb. At the summit is a small clearing with good views of the bald crest of Pine Mountain and the spruce covered summit of Virginia's highest peak, Mount Rogers. The crest of Second Peak is 1.8 miles from the trailhead.

The trail descends to the saddle between Second Peak and First Peak. Initially, the descent is moderate, but becomes easy. In this saddle chestnut oak, hemlock, and maple can be found. There are two trail junctions in this saddle. Shapiro Trail exits left (See Shapiro Trail description). Just past this junction, the Bearpen Trail exits right (See Bearpen Trail description). There is a large clearing and several camp areas. These trail junctions are reached at 2.4 miles

The trail climbs quickly to the crest of First Peak and then begins a gradual drop to a "T" trail junction. The Kabel Trail is to the right and the Hightree Rock Trail is to the left. The trail passes through a very scenic upland hardwood forest prior to reaching the trail. There is a sign for directions at the trail junction.

Little Wilson Creek Trail   6

Length: 1.7 Miles
Time: 2.25 Hours
Elevation Change: 800 Feet
Difficulty: Moderate
USGS Maps: Troutdale
Trailhead: Via the Big Wilson Creek/Kabel Trail

How To Get There

Travel to Grayson Highlands State Park. The park is located just off US 58 about 7.6 miles west from the intersections of US 16 and US 58. At the park entrance, turn right and follow the signs to the campground area. It is best to avoid CR 817 as this road is only passable by four wheel drive vehicles.

Trail Description

This description of Little Wilson Creek Trail begins at a bushwhack from Kaleb Trail. The trail can be accessed from CR 817, however, it crosses private property. The best use of the trail is part of a large circuit which includes the AT, Bearpen Trail, Big Wilson Creek Trail, and Kaleb Trail. From the Kaleb Trail, the Little Wilson Trail leads out of the wilderness to an old fire road. Then a short hike up Big Wilson Creek returns to the parking area. Little Wilson Creek Trail is absolutely beautiful and is a "must hike" in this wilderness area.

The trail begins at the meadow and creek on the Kaleb Trail (See Big Wilson/Kabel Trail description). If traveling along the Big Wilson/Kaleb Trail toward the First Peak Trail junction, take a right at the meadow and follow the creek south. The hike begins as a bushwhack. Stay on the left side of the stream. The trail follows Little Wilson Creek until it exits the wilderness area, so finding water to filter is not a problem. Within 0.2 miles after leaving the Kabel Trail, is a laurel thicket. Getting through the thicket requires stooping, ducking, and even crawling on hands and knees. The trail begins within .75 miles of Kaleb Trail.

The beginning of the actual trail is very rough. The route is visible because of downed trees which have been cut out of the way. The trail winds through boulders, rock outcoppings, and tall hemlock. The trail generally parallels the creek. Sometimes it is close to the creek and at other times veering away from the creek bank. The stream falls far below, the trail and large hemlock logs bridge its banks. Stay to the left of the stream. The trail is easy to follow but is rocky. This section will last for approximately 1.1 miles (approximately 1.8 miles from Kaleb Trail).

When the trail exits the wilderness and passes a large sign, look for another trail which exits to the right. Continuing straight leads to CR 817. The right trail leads to a swimming hole on Little Wilson Creek. After taking a dip, weather permitting, cross the stream. There should be an old apple orchard on the other side. Once in the orchard there is an overgrown fire road. Follow the road uphill (southeast) until reaching a powerline. At the powerline there is a right switchback. The fire road contours the mountainside, passes through hardwood forest, and leaves Little Wilson Creek behind. The road is easy to follow. A drainage stream is crossed. The trail contours the ridge and then climbs up hill with the first three switchbacks. The switchbacks are separated by long moderate grades, so the climb is not difficult. From the swimming hole, to the parking area is about 2.25 miles.

A cabin at the start of the Little Wilson Creek Trail.

Scales Trail   7

Length: 1.3 Miles
Time: 30 Minutes
Difficulty: Easy
Elevation Change: 250 Feet
USGS Maps: Troutdale
Trailhead: CR 613 and Grayson Highlands State Park

How To Get There

Travel to Grayson Highlands State Park. The park is located just off US 58, 7.6 miles west from the intersections of US 16 and US 58. At the park entrance, turn right and follow the signs to the campground area. There is a sign for the Wilson Creek Trail. The parking area is on the left near the campground store.

Take I-81 to Marion, Va. Take Exit #45 and turn south on US 16. Travel 17.2 miles and turn right on CR 603. Proceed 2.8 miles to CR 613 and turn left. Travel 3.7 miles to the Scales area. CR 613 is a rough road and not recommended for passenger cars.

Trail Description

The Scales Trail is a short horse trail leading from an area near the Grayson Highlands State Park to a saddle on Pine Mountain. The trail borders the western boundary of the wilderness for a short distance. The trail has many nice views of Pine Mountain and its surrounding meadows.

The trail begins at the end of a dirt road. Near the beginning of the trail, there is a small creek to cross. Shortly after crossing the creek, the AT crosses the Scales Trail (See AT description). There are many fine views of the Pine Mountain after the AT junction. At 0.5 miles is the junction with the Bearpen Trail. The Bearpen Trail exits right (See Bearpen Trail description). Approximately 0.8 miles beyond this junction, the Scales Trail connects with several other trails, including the First Peak Trail (See First Peak Trail description).

A view of Wilburn Ridge from the Scales Trail.

Shapiro Trail   8

Length: 3.2 Miles
Time: 2 Hours
Difficulty: Moderate
Elevation Change: 1,100 Feet
USGS Maps: Troutdale
Trailhead: CR 739

How To Get There

Take I-81 to Marion, Va. Take Exit #45 and turn south on US 16. Travel 17.2 miles and turn right on CR 603. Proceed 1.1 miles and turn left on CR 739. Proceed 0.9 miles to a parking area on the right. Remember not to block the gate.

Trail Description

The Shaprio Trail is a short trail from CR 739 to the saddle between First Peak and Second Peak. This trail provides quick access into the wilderness and the many trails therein. The 3.2 mile trail climbs quickly from the trailhead to the saddle. The trail passes through a forest of mixed hardwoods.

At the trailhead is a gate. Cross the gate and hike 1.7 miles up a road. At the wilderness boundary, there is a red gate. Just beyond

121

the gate is a trail sign with the distance to the saddle. Here the road ends and the trail begins. The trail starts with a moderate climb, which quickly becomes steep. Midway up the slope, there are some rocks on the right which provide a convenient spot to stop and rest. The trail climbs to an old road where the grade again becomes moderate. There is a small spring near this location. Finally, the trail becomes almost flat and enters a clearing. In this clearing is the junction with the First Peak Trail (See First Peak Trail description).

Wilson Creek Trail   9

Length: 1.4 Miles
Time: 45 Minutes
Difficulty: Easy/Moderate
Elevation Change: 800 Feet
USGS Maps: Troutdale
Trailhead: Grayson Highlands State Park

How To Get There

Travel to Grayson Highlands State Park. The park is located just off US 58, 7.6 miles west from the intersections of US 16 and US 58. At the park entrance, turn right and follow the signs to the campground area. There is a sign for the Wilson Creek Trail. The parking area is on the left near the campground store.

Trail Description

The Wilson Creek Trail follows Wilson Creek along the boundary of the wilderness and Grayson Highlands State Park. Wilson Creek is a fast flowing creek with many rock ledges and small waterfalls. The trail is short but provides a scenic access into the Wilson Creek Wilderness.

The trailhead, located on the left side of the road, is marked by a sign. The trail crosses a dirt road and drops rapidly to Wilson Creek. A left on this dirt road leads to the Scales Trail and the AT. The trail along the Wilson Creek eventually leads back to this road. At the creek, turn left and hike uphill. A side trail crosses the creek on a log bridge and leads to a small campsite in the wilderness. This bridge is slick so be careful when crossing. The grade of Wilson Creek Trail is not difficult with the exception of one short section which has a series of short ups and downs. One tree species of note is Frazier magnolia. There is a small rest area in the magnolia grove.

The trail makes a short, steep climb away from the creek and rejoins the road. A left on the road goes back to the trailhead while a right leads to the wilderness.

Mountain Lake Wilderness

Mountain Lake

Mountin Lake Wilderness is a 10,753 acre wilderness in the Blacksburg Ranger District of the Jefferson National Forest. The Mountain Lake Wilderness was created by Congress in 1984. The wilderness is located in Giles and Craig Counties, Virginia and Monroe County, West Virginia. Mountain Lake is the only wilderness in the state to cross state lines. The primitive area is approximately thirteen miles north of Blacksburg, Virginia.

The wilderness gets it name from Mountain Lake, a natural lake found at the top of Salt Pond Mountain. Mountain Lake Wilderness is also located at the top of Salt Pond Mountain and includes the eastern slope of the mountain. The eastern and western slopes of Potts Mountain are within the boundaries of the Mountain Lake Wilderness. Several small streams are located within the boundary of the wilderness. Some of the streams include Johns Creek, War Spur Branch, White Rocks Branch, Saltpeter Branch and Stoney Creek. Water is plentiful within the wilderness boundaries, but remember to always treat the water before drinking.

There is an extensive trail system within the boundaries of the Mountain Lake Wilderness. There are about twenty-five miles of trail located within the wilderness area. Most of the trails are well maintain and in good condition. Some of the trails, over in the West Virginia region, show light use and can be difficult to follow. The Virginia section of the wilderness area is a popular hiking area and used extensively. Therefore, if solitude is your goal, Mountain Lake may not be the place. For backpackers, there are many good places to camp along the trails and there is an Appalachian Trail shelter at the bottom of Salt Pond Mountain near Johns Creek.

Salt Pond Mountain is over 4,300 feet high, and because of the high elevation, red spruce can be found in small pockets. There is a small stand of virgin timber located at the upper reaches of the War Spur Branch. Yellow Birch, hemlock, and red spruce dominate this high valley. The rest of the mountain is covered by the oak-hickory ecosystem which dominates much of Virginia's mountains. There are old pastures located throughout the wilderness. Many of these old pastures are slowly being reclaimed by the forest. In these area, small locust and even some cedar can be found.

There are several interesting locations in the wilderness area. Manns bog is a wet area which provides the springs for the headwaters of Little Stony Creek. Huge ferns fields co-exist along side large hemlocks and red spruce. The are several rock outcrops located

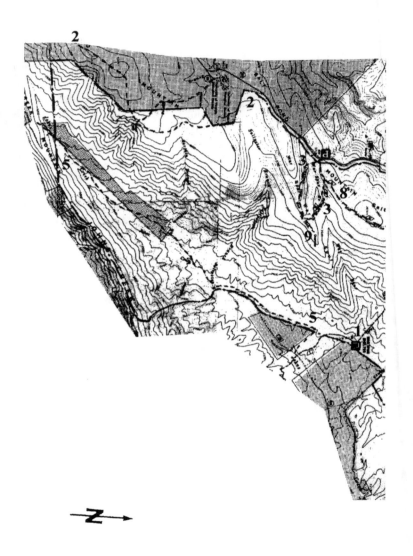

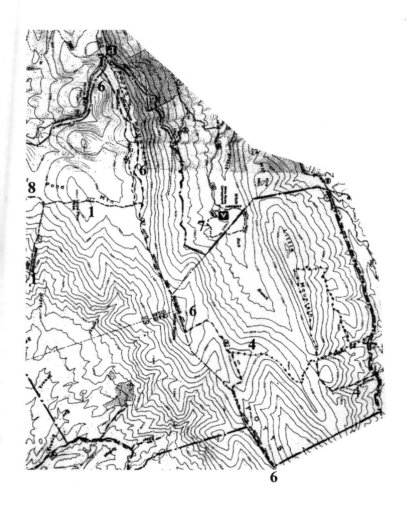

throughout the wilderness. All of the outcrops provide excellent views of the surrounding countryside. The White Rocks, War Spur Overlook, Bear Cliffs and Wind Rock are a few of the outcrops located in Mountain Lake Wilderness. Finally, as mentioned earlier, Mountain Lake also has an easily accessible stand of virgin timber. These huge trees are found in the sheltered cove of War Spur Branch and are reached via the Chestnut Trail. The Chestnut Trail is an easy hike for most people.

Note: CR 700 changes to CR 613 at the Mountain Lake Resort.

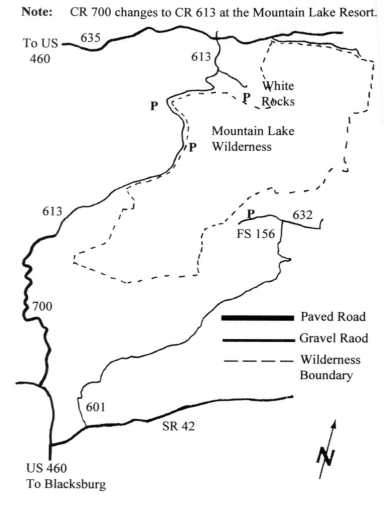

Appalachian Trail   1

Length: 4.6 Miles (One Way)
Time: 2.25 Hours
Difficulty: Moderate/Difficult
Elevation Change: 2,000 Feet
USGS Maps: Interior and Waiteville
Trailhead: CR 613 and FS 156

How To Get There

Take I-81 to Exit #121. Take US 460 West toward Blacksburg.
At Blacksburg, take the US 460 bypass around Blacksburg. At the
junction of 460 West and the 460 bypass, west of Blacksburg, travel
6.6 miles to the CR 700 and turn right. There is a sign for Mountain
Lake at the intersection. Travel 6.9 miles to the Mountain Lake Resort. CR 700 changes to CR 613 at the resort. Travel 4.0 miles to a
parking area on the left. This parking area is just before the road
begins to descend down the mountain.
To the Johns Creek parking area Take I-81 to Exit #121. Take
US 460 West toward Blacksburg. At Blacksburg, take the US 460
bypass around Blacksburg. At the junction of 460 West and the 460
bypass, west of Blacksburg, travel 5.0 miles to SR 42 and turn right.
Travel 1.0 miles and turn left on CR 601. AT 0.8 miles is a "Y"
intersection, bear right and continue 7.2 miles to CR 632. At 4.6
miles CR 601 turn into a gravel road. At CR 632, turn left and proceed 0.7 miles to a parking area on the right.

Trail Description

The AT travels through the heart of the Mountain Lake Wilderness Area. This portion of the trail begins near the top of Salt Pond
Mountain and makes its way to the bottom of the mountain. The AT
leaves the wilderness near the War Spur Shelter and before crossing
FS 156. The path is marked with the distinctive white blazes of the
AT. The trail winds through open glades and fern fields. The forest
species range from evergreens such as hemlock, white pine, and red
spruce to hardwoods like red and white oak, hickory, locust, maple,
and poplar. The trail is long, making it a difficult out and back.
At the beginning of the trail is a Forest Service information center. There are two trails in this area, but both lead to the same location. The ATclimbs at an easy grade to a small clearing at Wind

Rock. There is a good view of Peters Mountain from this rock out-crop. The Potts Mountain Trail bears to the left at the boulder barrier (See Potts Mountain Trail description). The AT is located more to the right. After leaving the clearing the AT is very flat. Shortly after leaving the clearing there is a small sign for a horse trail which crosses the AT. This trail shows little use.

The trail enters an old clearing covered with young locust trees. About fifty yards to the left is a small clearing which makes an excellent campsite. The trail makes a short steep drop with a left switchback. After the switchback there is a more gradual decline followed by another gradual incline. A small trail intersects the AT from the left. This trail leads to a "T" intersection with the Potts Mountain Trail. Just beyond this intersection is a fern field which is covered with ferns and tall hemlock.

Next, the trail starts a steep drop. The AT intersects with the War Spur Connector Trail (See War Spur Connector Trail description). A sign at this intersection indicates that the War Spur Trail is 1.5 miles long. Hiking back to the trailhead is 2.6 miles and to the War Spur Shelter is 1.3 miles. The trees consist of large oak, hickory, maple, and white pine.

The trail continues its steep drop to the War Spur Shelter. As the region becomes drier, chestnut oak, Virginia pine, and mountain laurel are the dominate species. About halfway between the War Spur Connector Trail and the AT shelter, there is an overlook with good views up the valley formed by Johns Creek and Johns Creek Mountain.

Shortly after the sounds of the War Spur Branch become audible, the AT reaches the War Spur shelter. At the shelter, is a sign for Johns Creek Mountain Trail and the distance back to CR 613 which is 3.9 miles. The trail turns to the right and crosses the War Spur Branch. On the other side of the branch, the trail becomes flat and easy. There is a small wilderness sign, and the trail exits the forest at FS 156. At 4.6 miles the trail meets the road.

Bear Cliffs Trail   2

Length: 3.9 Miles (One Way)
Time: 2 Hours
Difficulty: Moderate
Elevation Change: 600 Feet
USGS Maps: Interior, Eggleston
Trailhead: CR 613

A view from the War Spur Overlook.

How To Get There

Take I-81 to Exit #121. Take 460 West toward Blacksburg. At Blacksburg, take the US 460 bypass around Blacksburg. At the junction of US 460 West and the US 460 bypass, west of Blacksburg, travel 6.6 miles to the CR 700 and turn right. There is a sign for Mountain Lake at the intersection. Travel 6.9 miles to the Mountain Lake Resort. CR 700 changes to CR 613 at the Resort. Travel 3.1 miles to the parking area for the War Spur Trail and hike back 0.7 miles to the trailhead.

Trail Description

This trail travels across the back of Salt Pond Mountain to the Bear Cliffs. The Bear Cliffs are huge rock outcrops which provide a great view to the east. The trail goes past the Bear Cliffs to the Mountain Lake Resort and the top of Bald Knob. It is marked with yellow blazes. Across the top of Salt Pond Mountain are huge fern fields created by many small springs. The area beyond Bear Cliffs is covered with short twisted oaks. All in all this is a great hike.

The trailhead is not marked, look for 2 poles in the ground, a posted sign, and a small wilderness sign. From the trailhead, cross an earth barrier and enter the woods. The trail is hard to see so watch for the yellow blazes. The first part of the trail is covered with grass and leaves, and many small trees line the path. The trail climbs to the top of a small knoll and the grade is easy. At the top, the trail becomes more visible and drops down the other side of the knoll. However, although more visible, it is still hard to see - watch for the yellow blazes.

After about 0.5 miles, the trail intersects with a trail called the Rhododendron Trail. The Rhododendron Trail exits to the left. There is a small sign at this intersection. Follow the Spruce Bog Trail and the Crossroads Trail. These trails are utilized by the UVA Biological Research Station, and throughout the region signs of research activity are evident. Remember not to disturb anything. Just beyond this trail junction, is a fern field with ferns almost waist high. It is a beautiful sight. At the next trail intersection, continue straight, the sign points toward Spruce Bog and the Crossroads Trail. Continue straight at the next trail intersection. Then at the trail crossroads, continue straight again. This is the last trail intersection.

After the last intersection, the trail goes though a series of easy ups and downs in a large fern field. The trees, mainly red oak, are much larger. After crossing Surtain Creek, about 1.3 miles from the trailhead, the trail begins to climb. Surtain Creek is the last place to find water along the trail. Remember to treat or filter the water. The climb to the Bear Cliffs area is about 0.7 miles. Initially, the grade is moderate and the forest is composed mainly of stunted red oaks. After a climb of about 0.5 miles, the trail becomes much easier. It winds through a rocky section and then enters the Bear Cliffs. There is a small trail to the left which leads to the cliffs. The Bear Cliffs are huge slabs of broken rock on the east side of Salt Pond Mountain. These cliffs provide a commanding view of Johns Creek, Johns Creek Mountain, and Brushy Mountain.

At the Bear Cliffs, the trail turns right and climbs for a short distance. When it levels out, a trail exits right. This trail leads to the Biological Research Station. There is also a sign at this junction for Mountain Lake and Bald Knob. The trail climbs gradually through a forest of small stunted red oak. Just beyond a short descent through a small boulder field, there is another trail junction. This junction is approximately 2.8 miles from the beginning of the trail. A trail exit right and descends toward Mountain Lake. There is a sign indicating trails which can be hiked near the Mountain Lake Resort. The grade is still easy and much of the path is bordered by grass and ferns.

The path terminates at a road leading to the top of Bald Knob. There is a sign here indicating the distance to the Bear Cliffs as 1.9

miles and the Biological Research Station as 2.8 miles. There is also a stone bench forresting weary bones. A right leads to the Mountain Lake Resort and a left leads to the summit of Bald Knob.

Chestnut Trail   3

Length: 2.5 Miles
Time: 1.5 Hours
Difficulty: Easy
Elevation Change: 250 Feet
USGS Maps: Interior
Trailhead: CR 613

How to Get There

Take I-81 to Exit #121. Take US 460 West toward Blacksburg. At Blacksburg, that the US 460 bypass around Blacksburg. At the junction of US 460 West and the US 460 bypass, west of Blacksburg, travel 6.6 miles to the CR 700 and turn right. There is a sign for Mountain Lake at the intersection. Travel 6.9 miles to the Mountain Lake Resort. CR 700 changes to CR 613 at the Resort. Travel 3.1 miles to a parking area on the right.

Trail Description

The Chestnut Trail is a short loop trail of about 2.5 miles in length. The trail travels through a mixed forest of hardwoods such as red oak, white oak, hickory, and maple. The trail also passes through a great stand of virgin hemlock, red spruce, and yellow poplar. This trail also connects with the War Spur Overlook Trail which has a commanding view of the War Spur Branch watershed and Johns Mountain.

The trail begins at a parking area located on the right side of CR 613. There is a wooden sign describing the names and lengths of the trails. The Chestnut Trail is the trail which exits right. From the trailhead to the War Spur Overlook Trail is 1.0 mile. The timber stand is approximately 0.25 miles beyond the trail junction.

The first part of the trail is a gradual downhill to a small creek. There is a campsite located on the right about 100 yards from the beginning of the trail. The trail crosses a bridge and begin a slow climb. There are many large red oaks and yellow poplars. The trail reaches a high point and begins a gradual descent. A small sign marks the junction of the War Spur Overlook Trail and the Chestnut Trail (See War Spur Overlook Trail description).

From here, the trail begin a steep descent to a stand of virgin timber. There is a right switchback and a left switchback. After the left switchback, the trail enters a rhododendron tunnel. On the other side of the tunnel, there is a beautiful stand of large and old red spruce and yellow birch. There is a small clearing in the timber stand and camping is prohibited. Virgin stands of timber are a rare sight in America today. The trail crosses a small log bridge before climbing out of the ancient grove.

The trail climbs at a more moderate pace leaving the old trees behind and entering a mixed stand of hardwood. The trail is grassy. About 1.0 miles beyond the timber stand, the Chestnut Trail intersects with the War Spur Trail. A right on the War Spur goes to the AT, while a left on the War Spur goes back to the parking lot (See War spur Connector Trail description).

Cut Hollow Trail/Bushwhack   4

Length: 2.2 Miles (One Way)
Time: 1.5 Hours
Difficulty: Difficult
Elevation Change: 1,280 Feet
USGS Maps: Interior, Waiteville
Trailhead: CR 635

How To Get There

Take I-81 to Exit #121. Take US 460 West toward Blacksburg. At Blacksburg, take the US 460 bypass around Blacksburg. At the junction of US 460 West and the US 460 bypass, west of Blacksburg, travel 16 miles to CR 635. Proceed 18 miles, entering West Virginia, to a parking area on the right.

Trail Description

The Cut Hollow Trail is found on most maps of the Mountain Lake Wilderness. The "trail" can be very difficult to follow and is recommended to those who are confident in their orienteering skills. There is a trail at the base of Little Mountain which is easy to follow, and the Potts Mountain Trail runs across the top of Potts Mountain.

A trail junction? on the Cut Hollow Trail.

The Cut Hollow Trail is a path between these two trails; a route from the base of the mountain to the top. The trail is difficult to find, overgrown in sections, and at times difficult to follow. Unless the trail is cleaned up significantly, expect to forge your own way.

The trail begins at a gate just off of CR 635. The pulloff is on the right. This section of trail is wide, flat, and easy to follow. If a leisurely stroll is desired this is the place to go. This relaxed mode ends at Cut Hollow.

Approximately 2.0 miles into the walk, at a right bend, the trail intersects with Cut Hollow. Most maps show two trails coming off the mountain. It is best to look for the second of the two. Keep an eye to the right of the trail. The trail climbs up the left side of a creek and then crosses over to the right. If the main trail (the wide flat one) becomes overgrown with small pine trees, turn around and look for the Cut Hollow Trail.

After finding Cut Hollow Trail, it is easy to follow. There is a moderately difficult climb up the mountain which levels off on a finger ridge. At this level spot be on the look for a trail on the left. This intersection is overgrown. The junction is just beyond a right bend in an area where the trail descends slightly.

Turn left at this intersection and begin climbing again. A right loops back to the first trail. While climbing up the mountain the trail becomes harder to follow and the grade is difficult. There are sections of visible trail and sections where the trail disappears altogether. Often, the trail is a wide, fern-covered old road. After a long right bend, the path becomes difficult to follow. With some bushwhacking and possibly a compass, the climb continues up the ridge. Eventually the Cut Hollow Trail/Bushwhack intersects with the Potts Mountain Trail.

A reminder: this bushwhack is difficult. It is described because most maps show a good trail through this area, and the Cut Hollow Trail connects two pleasant trails. The path is overgrown and following the trail can be difficult. The ridges and hollows can be confusing and becoming lost is not out of the realm of possibility.

Johns Creek   5

Length: 3.7 Miles (One Way)
Time: 2 Hours
Difficulty: Easy
Elevation Change: 900 Feet
USGS Maps: Eggleston, Waiteville, Newport
Trailhead: CR 632

How To Get There

Take I-81 to Exit #121. Take US 460 West toward Blacksburg. At Blacksburg, that the US 460 bypass around Blacksburg. At the junction of US 460 West and the US 460 bypass, west of Blacksburg, travel 5.0 miles to SR 42 and turn right. Travel 1.0 miles and turn left on CR 601. AT 0.8 miles is a "Y" intersection, bear right and continue 7.2 miles to CR 632. At 4.6 miles CR 601 turn into a gravel road. At CR 632, turn left and proceed 0.7 miles to a parking area on the right.

Trail Description

The Johns Creek Trail is a long "out and back" through the Johns Creek drainage basin. The trail climbs slowly from parking area to the powerlines located on the southern edge of the wilderness. The trail has only a few short inclines, climbing from 2,100 feet to 3,000 feet over 4.2 miles.

Forest species along the trail include, mixed hardwoods such as oak, hickory, maple, and tulip poplar. Hemlock and white pine are interspersed among the hardwoods. The understory includes species such as striped maple, dogwood, rhododendron, and laurel.

The parking area is located on the right side of the road. Walk southwest past the Applachain Trail. On the right just past the AT, there is an old road and a small sign stating "wilderness access road". The road is easy to follow with many red Forest Service boundary blazes on the trees. The trail blazes are yellow. The first portion of the trail leads around a small section of private property. There is an easy uphill grade as the trail snakes through a typical mixed hardwood forest.

The path crosses a small creek and begins an easy descent to Johns Creek. At a "T" intersection with an old road, turn left and continue downhill. A right on this road leads to a dead end or for the adventurous hiker a bushwhack up the mountain. The trail/road joins another old road. At this junction, turn right. A left leads back to private property. Johns Creek is on the left. The junction is 1.2 miles from the trailhead. Throughout this area is a mixture of cove hardwoods, hemlocks, and beautiful ferns.

The trail crosses three small streams and the larger Saltpeter Creek tumbles down Salt Pond Mountain. After the creek crossing, the trail begins to climb, however the grade is still easy. The trail passes through a rhododendron thicket and Johns Creek is on the left. Just beyond the thicket, on the left bank of Johns Creek is a great campsite.

At 2.4 miles, the Johns Creek trail crosses Surtain Creek and just beyond the creek is a small clearing with a large three forked locust tree. The next clearing has lots of trash and an old bedspring for rest, if necessary. The trail, which passes to the right of the clearing, continues to climb. On the other side of the clearing, the trail is used less and more brushy. The walking is more difficult but not impossible. After a short distance, another small creek crosses the trail and just beyond this creek are the powerlines. The trail goes under the lines and slowly fizzles out. The wilderness appropriately enough ends at the power lines.

Potts Mountain Trail   6

Length: 5.1 Miles (One Way)
Time: 2 Hours
Elevation Change: 720 Feet
Difficulty: Easy
USGS Map: Interior, Waiteville
Trailhead: CR 613

A fine bridge across a stream.

How To Get There

Take I-81 to Exit #121. Take US 460 West toward Blacksburg. At Blacksburg, that the US 460 bypass around Blacksburg. At the junction of US 460 West and the US 460 bypass, west of Blacksburg, travel 6.6 miles to the CR 700 and turn right. There is a sign for Mountain Lake at the intersection. Travel 6.9 miles to the Mountain Lake Resort. CR 700 changes to County Route 613 at the resort. Travel 4.0 miles to a parking area on the left. This parking area is just before the road begins to descend down the mountain.

Trail Description

The Potts Mountain Trail is a very pleasant, easy hike offering a wide variety of interesting sights and sounds. The trail passes panoramic vistas, high mountain balds, and rock outcroppings. The area is prime for various types of wildlife and bird sightings. The only negative comments about this trail are the fact that there is little water available, and the hike is an out-and-back with limited options for a circuit hike.

From the parking lot for the AT, follow the AT about .25 miles to the Wind Rock. There is a campsite near the rocky outcrop. From the camping area the AT (See AT description) branches to the right while the Potts Mountain Trail continues straight . The trail is wide and easy to follow. There are sections of rock to the left. At about 0.8 miles the trail passes through a small open area. This open space is an excellent location for camping. Just remember to pack in water.

The next landmark is a small rock wall on the left. Near this wall, the trail starts an easy descent followed by an equally easy ascent. At slightly more than 1.1 miles is a large, open bald. The trail stays on the left side of this field. After the bald, there is an easy descent. Keep an eye out for a white blaze because the trail passes an AT spur at about 1.8 miles. The Spur exits the trail to the right.

From the intersection with the AT spur, the trail continues this easy grade until wrapping around a large set of rocks. The Potts Mountain Trail continues out to the crest of the ridge, passing more rocks, this time on the right. This area is called White Rocks and here it is possible to climb the rocks and get a beautiful view of the War Spur Branch, Johns Mountain, and Bald Knob. At slightly less than 3.6 miles, the trail reaches the edge of the ridgetop and begins a steep descent. This is the best place to turn around and head back as the trail soon leaves wilderness.

If you choose to go on, the trail turns left and descends down the ridge. At 3.8 miles the trail bends right. Approximately 4.2 miles from the trailhead, the Potts Mountain Trail intersects with the Cut Hollow Trail/Bushwhack (See Cut Hollow Trail/Bushwhack description). Just beyond this junction, the trail turns right and climbs back to the ridgetop. Once on the ridgetop, the trail makes a left turn and heads out of the wilderness. This wilderness boundary is about 5.1 miles from the beginning of the trail.

Virginia's Trail   7

Length: 1.3 Miles
Time: 45 Minutes
Difficulty: Easy
Elevation Change: 100 Feet
USGS Maps: Waiteville
Trailhead: White Rocks Recreation Area

How To Get There

Take I-81 to Exit #121. Take US 460 West toward Blacksburg. At Blacksburg, that the US 460 bypass around Blacksburg. At the junction of US 460 West and the US 460 bypass, west of Blacksburg, travel 16 miles to CR 635 and turn right. Travel 15.2 miles to CR 613 and turn right. Travel 0.7 miles to the entrance to the White Rocks Recreation Area on the left. If the gate is open travel approximately 0.8 miles to the Recreation Area, turn right and look for the sign for Virginia's Trail.

Trail Description

This trail is a short 1.3 mile trail from the White Rocks Recreation Area into the Mountain Lake Wilderness and then back to the recreation area. The trail is a loop that wanders through a mixed hardwood forest. If the gates are locked another 1.6 miles should be added to the length of the hike.

The trail begins at the Virginia's Trail sign. This easy trail starts out with a very gradual incline for about 0.25 miles, and then drops down into a small creek bottom. The trail crosses this small creek two times. Both crossings are made on log bridges. Paralleling the creek the trail begins a long gradual descent to an area of hemlock and rhododendron. Before reaching the evergreens, there is a sign marking the halfway point. Once in the hemlock forest, there is a bridge which crosses a wide, calm creek.

The trail climbs out of the creek bottom and forms the boundary line between the hemlock and rhododendron forest on the left and the oak-hickory forest on the right. The trail enters a small field and crosses the creek again, this time on a short board walk. The White Rocks Recreation Area is at the end of the boardwalk. The trail ends in the recreation area near campsite 31.

War Spur Connector Trail   8

Length: 1.5 Miles (One Way)
Time: 45 Minutes
Difficulty: Easy
Elevation Change: 100 Feet
USGS Maps: Interior, Waiteville
Trailhead: CR 613

How to Get There

Take I-81 to Exit #121. Take US 460 West toward Blacksburg. At Blacksburg, that the US 460 bypass around Blacksburg. At the junction of US 460 west and the US 460 bypass, west of Blacksburg, travel 6.6 miles to the CR 700 and turn right. There is a sign for Mountain Lake at the intersection. Travel 6.9 miles to the Mountain Lake Resort. CR 700 changes to CR 613 at the Resort. Travel 3.1 miles to a parking area on the right.

<u>Trail Description</u>

This trail connects the Chestnut Trail to the AT and provides easy access to the AT. This easy trail is about 1.5 miles long. The forest is comprised of hardwoods such as red oak, chestnut oak, and hickory. There are also evergreens such as Virginia pine, white pine, and hemlock.

The trail begins at a parking area on the right side of CR 613 near the top of Salt Pond Mountain. The trailhead for both the Chestnut Trail and War Spur Trail are located in this parking area. There is a big wooden sign describing the trails at the trailhead. The War Spur Trail exits left.

The War Spur Trail begins as a wide, grassy, flat trail. At 0.3 miles it intersects with the Chestnut Trail. The Chestnut Trail exits right (See Chestnut Trail description). After this intersection, the War Spur Trail begins a very gradual climb followed by a long gradual descent. There are many tall oak trees in the region.

At 1.1 miles the trail begins a moderate descent. Mountain laurel and pine dominate this slope. After passing a small wet area on the right, the trail begins a steep, rocky descent. Just before reaching the AT, the War Spur Trail levels out. There is a sign marking the junction with the AT (See AT description).

War Spur Overlook Trail   9

Length: 0.25 Miles
Time: 10 Minutes
Difficulty: Easy
Elevation Change: 60 Feet
USGS Maps: Interior, Waiteville
Trailhead: Via the Chestnut Trail

<u>How to Get There</u>

Via the Chestnut Trail

Trail Description

The War Spur Overlook Trail is a short trail, 0.2 miles in length, leading from the Chestnut Trail to the War Spur Overlook. The trail is accessed via the Chestnut Trail (See Chestnut Trail description). From the Chestnut Trail/War Spur Overlook Trail junction, the War Spur Overlook Trail begins an easy descent. Prior to reaching the overlook there is a campsite on the right. The rock outcrop overlooks the War Spur Branch and provides an excellent view of the mighty hemlock and red spruce of the War Spur's virgin stand of timber. The White Rocks outcrop is visible on Potts Mountain. There is also a good view of Johns Mountain to the east.

Peters Mountain Wilderness

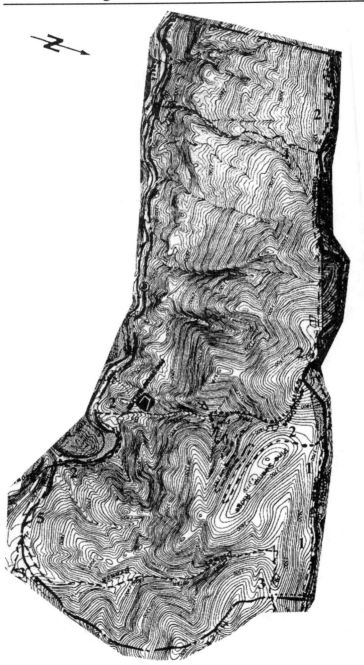

Peters Mountain

Peters Mountain is a small wilderness located on the Virginia-West Virginia border. The wilderness is located approximately nineteen miles west of Blacksburg, Virginia. This roadless area located in the Blacksburg District of the Jefferson National Forest occupies an area of approximately 3,326 acres. Peters Mountain was declared a wilderness by Congress in 1984.

The Peters Mountain Wilderness, not surprisingly, is located on the eastern slope of Peters Mountain. The ridge of Peters Mountain forms the western boundary of the wilderness area. Stony Creek and County Route 635 form the eastern boundary. Within the wilderness area are two small creeks. The first is Dismal Branch which empties into the Little Stony Creek. The second creek is Pine Swamp Branch which empties into the Stony Creek.

There are several trails throughout the Peters Mountain Wilderness Area. There are appoximately twenty miles of trail in and around the wilderness area. All of the trails are well maintained with few natural obstacles. Most trails start at a creek bottoms and climb up the side of the mountain. This creates some strenuous hikes. Water is abundant during the climbs up the ridge because many of the trails run along the small streams which flow down Peters Mountain. However, always remember to treat the water before drinking. There is one Appalachian Trail shelter within the wilderness boundaries.

The forest of Peters Mountain Wilderness varies widely in age. There is one small pocket of virgin hemlock and red spruce in the Peters Mountain Wilderness Area located on the side of the mountain near to the ridge top. The crest is dominated by storm damaged chestnut oak and other hardy species. The forest of the eastern slope of the mountain is composed of the oak-hickory ecosystem. Finally, in the creek bottoms and the sheltered coves there are stands of hemlock, white pine, and yellow birch. Near the headwaters of Dismal Creek is a large, dense rhododendron thicket. Fortunately, there is a trail through the thicket.

The area seems to see heavy use. Therefore, if you are seeking solitude the best time to hike this area is during the winter months. Otherwise, expect to see hikers and backpackers on your visit to the area. In the spring and fall the area sees heavy use by students from Virginia Tech.

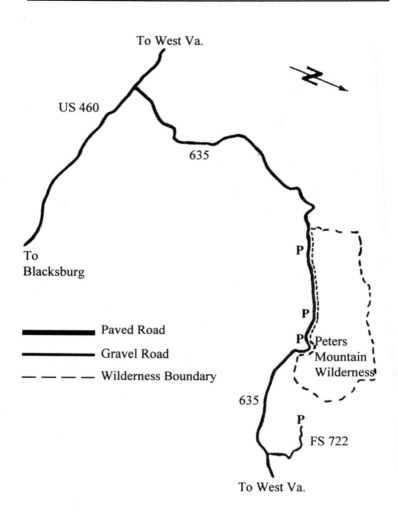

Allegheny Trail 1

Length: 1.3 Miles (One Way)
Time: 45 Minutes
Difficulty: Easy
Elevation Change: 100 Feet
USGS Maps: Interior
Trailhead: Via the AT

How To Get There

Via the AT or the Flat Peter Trail

Trail Description

The Allegheny Trail is a 330 mile trail along the crest of the Allegheny Mountains. Through the Peters Mountain Wilderness, the trail is marked with yellow blazes and varies from a narrow footpath to a road suitable for four wheel drive vehicles. Along the crest of Peters Mountain, the trail tracks the western boundary of the Peters Mountain Wilderness. There is a great deal of storm damage at the top of the mountain, but it does not interfere with hiking. Initially, the trail/road is well maintained and easy to follow. However, toward the end it becomes a road for four wheeled vehicles and can be very muddy.

The trail begins near the crest of Peters Mountain at the junction with the Appalachian Trail. At this junction is a sign with information about the Allegheny Trail. At this junction, turn right and follow the yellow blazes. Initially, the trail is a small path, but quickly changes into a four wheeler trail winding around trees and brush along the top of the mountain. About 0.8 miles from the junction with the AT, the Allegheny Trail becomes a rutted, muddy mess.

After a distance of 1.3 miles, a small wilderness sign is visible on the right side of the trail. This sign marks the nothern boundary of the wilderness area. At this location, one has the option to continue along the Allegheny Trail. By turning right and hiking down the mountain, a short bushwack of about 0.4 miles leads to the Flat Peter Trail (See Flat Peter Loop Trail description). Finally, there is always the backtrack to the original starting point.

Appalachian Trail   2

Length: 8.2 Miles
Time: 4.5 Hours
Difficulty: Difficult
Elevation Change: 1,420 Feet
USGS Maps: Interior, Lindside
Trailheads: CR 635

How To Get There

There are two ways to access the wilderness via the AT. Take I-81 to Exit #121. Follow US 460 West to Blacksburg. After the intersection of US 460 Bypass and US 460 Business just west of Blackburg, travel 16 miles to CR 635. Turn right on CR 635 and proceed 9.8 miles to a parking area on the left side of the road. There is a bridge just after the parking area. The AT also crosses CR 635 another 1.7 miles further up the road. This description begins where the AT crosses CR 635. The best place to park is at the Cherokee Flats a parking area about 0.1 miles further up the road.

Trail Description

The AT through the Peters Mountain Wilderness is a very scenic trail. The trail travels from CR 635 along Stony Creek, up the mountain, and then across the ridge top. As is typical with the AT, the trail makes no bones about getting to the top of the ridge - the climb is difficult. The climb is worth the effort, though, as the hiker is rewarded with beautiful views into West Virginia from nearly 4000 feet. As always, the AT is marked with white blazes.

Where the AT crosses CR 635, it enters the woods on the west side of the road. This is the same side as the Cherokee Flats parking area. The trail crosses Stony Creek and enters a region with large rhododendron and hemlock. The trail continues along at an easy grade for about 0.5 miles and then begins a moderate climb up to a finger ridge. It then drops quickly and connects to a wide, old road grade at 0.9 miles.

The AT turns to the right. A left leads back to the Stony Creek - a distance of about 0.25 miles with a difficult creek crossing. This trail is very flat as it parallels the Dismal Branch. The AT turns to the left after about 0.25 miles and crosses the Dismal Branch on a little foot bridge. FS Trail 268 continues on straight to the Flat Peter

Loop Trail (See FS Trail 268 description). After crossing the bridge there is a small open area and a campsite.

Just past the campsite, the AT bends to the left and again parallels the Dismal Branch. The area is flat and the hiking is easy. The trail enters a series of steep ups and downs which can be tiring, especially after a full day of hiking. The last climb has a switch to the left, and after the switch, the trail bends to the right and makes a steep drop down to Stony Creek. Here the AT becomes relatively flat. Just before entering a rhododendron tunnel, the trail crosses a small branch. A small sign indicates a distance of 0.8 miles to the Pine Swamp Shelter. On the other side of the tunnel the trail connects with the other AT parking area approximately 2.4 miles south of the Cherokee Flats parking area. There is a Forest Service information center at the parking area.

The Pine Swamp AT Shelter

AT From the Lower Parking Area

This section of the AT can be accessed from a parking lot just to the near the bridge on CR 635. The Forest Service information center may erroneously give the distance to the Alleghany Trail intersection as 1.3 miles. This was apparently the case with the "old" route the AT took through the wilderness. Now the distance is closer to 2.5 miles, but the junction of the AT and the Allegheny Trail is still in the same place. The extra mileage is due to a series of switchbacks that travel up the ridge.

From the parking area follow the trail about twenty yards and make a left. The trail climbs up the ridge and away from the creek. The Pine Swamp Shelter is about 0.25 miles from the Forest Service information center. The forest through here is predominately hardwoods and rhododendron. After passing the shelter, the grade becomes more difficult and the trail is rocky. A small mountain creek is on the right. At about 1.0 miles there is a fork in the trail. The "old" AT is the left arm of the fork. This trail is not recommended as there is great deal of downed timber. This old trail is now in the process of being reclaimed by nature. Take the right fork to remain on the AT. If confused about the right direction, look for the white blazes. Also remember - the AT is <u>very</u> well maintained. If this isn't the case you are probably not on the AT.

After the fork the AT crosses a dry creek bed and climbs the Pine Swamp Ridge with a series of about 15 switchbacks. The length between switchbacks increases as the trail gets closer to the ridge top. About 2.0 miles into the hike, the trail wraps around Pine Swamp Ridge and then travels down through a saddle between two ridges. The AT connects with the Allegheny Trail in this small saddle near the crest of the mountain. This junction is approximately 2.5 miles from CR 635. There is a sign at this intersection giving directions and distances. The Groundhog Trail is 3.9 miles away and US 460 is 16.9 miles away.

To continue along the AT, take a left at the junction and travel south towards the Groundhog Trail. A right at the junction heads in the direction of the Allegheny Trail (See Allegheny Trail description). The AT contours along the west side of the ridge top and there are views into West Virginia when the leaves are down. Previous maps of the area show the trail crossing the 3,956 foot summit of Peters Mountain. The trail actually passes to the west of this summit. The trees on the ridge are mostly hardwoods. There is a great deal of downed timber and many small, knotted trees - evidence of long, hard winters. The local AT club must be very active and dedicated, though, as there is little downfall blocking the trail.

At 4.0 miles the trail passes to the west of another peak and then starts down. The grade is moderate. There are many large boulders on the east side of the trail near the ridge top. When the trail tops the ridge, there are views to the east as well as to the west. The trail drops quickly to the Dickenson Gap, approximately 5.4 miles, and reaches the junction with the Groundhog Trail (See Groundhog Trail description). The Groundhog Trail exits the AT to the left and begins to descend rapidly.

From the intersection with the Groundhog Trail the wilderness hiker has a few options. One is to continue on the AT until it reaches the western edge of the wilderness area (or until you get to Georgia if that's what you want). A second is to turn around and retrace your steps back to the parking lot from where the hike began. A third option is to follow the blue-blazed Groundhog Trail off the mountain and then travel the road back to the parking area. From the intersection with the Groundhog Trail, the AT climbs a steep hill to the ridge top and exits the wildernesss. The wilderness boundary is 7.2 miles from the CR 635. The climb is worth the effort as there are some nice views and some interesting rocks. However, since US 460 is over 10 miles away, continuing south on the AT is a "backpacking only" adventure.

A recommendation for the dayhiker: When the intersection with the Groundhog Trail is reached climb the steep section and have a seat on the rocks and enjoy the scenery. From here walk back down, follow the Groundhog Trail's express route off the mountain (take it slow to prevent knee stress), and then follow the paved road back to the original parking area. The walk along the paved road is a little long but does follow a trout stream and you can swap a lie with a fisherman or two.

The AT at the crest of Potts Mountain.

Flat Peter Trail   3

Length: 8.8 Miles
Time: 4.5 Hours
Difficulty: Moderate
Elevation Change: 1,000 Feet
USGS Maps: Interior
Trailhead: FS 722

How To Get There

Take I-81 to Exit #121. Follow US 460 West to Blacksburg. After the intersection of US 460 Bypass and US 460 Business just west of Blackburg, travel 16 miles to CR 635. Turn right on CR 635 and proceed 13.4 miles to FS 722 and turn left. Travel 0.25 miles to the gate. Remember not to block the gate.

Trail Description

This is an 8.8 mile loop trail through Kellys Flat, up Dismal Branch, and returning to the starting point along Dixon Branch. The trail is marked with yellow blazes and includes excellent examples of the plant life located in this region.

The best way to hike this trail is counter clockwise. Therefore, from the parking area walk back down to the road on the right. Turn right and cross the gate. The first 2.1 miles follows a road through a narrow meadow, that is lined on both sides by tall white pine, oak, and maple. Many tall ferns and rhododendron line the meadows edge. The trail is basically flat and the grade is easy. About 0.7 miles the road bends right and crosses a small creek. On the right is a large swampy bog. After the bog the Flat Peter Trail enters an area of recent logging activity.

Next, the trail wanders through an area that was logged over many years ago. This area is covered with many small dogwoods and pine trees. The ground is covered with blueberry plants. The trail exits the clearing at 1.8 miles and enters the forest. A short distance after entering the forest there is a wide trail junction. The junction is 2.1 miles from the trailhead. The Flat Peter Trail turns right, while the straight fork is FS Trail 268 which leads to the AT (See FS Trail 268 description). The trees in this region are mainly small hardwoods. After the junction the trail begins to climb, but the grade is still easy. The Dismal Branch is on the left and the vegetation changes from an oak-hickory forest to one dominated by hemlock, white pine, white oak, and rhododendron.

Just before the first of ten creek crossings, approximately 0.5 miles from the junction, there is a small clearing on the right. This clearing is flat and is an excellent campsite. After crossing the creek two times the grade becomes more moderate. The foliage is lush and the forest is beautiful. The trail makes two more easy crossings of the creek. After the second crossing, there is a great deal of storm damage which makes the hiking more difficult. While climbing through the damage, the creek is crossed again, but the creek is now under a large pile of rocks and can only be heard.

After this crossing, the trail enters a beautiful garden of large ferns and yellow birch. About 1.0 miles from the junction, the trail crosses the creek again and becomes steeper. Following this short steep section the trail flattens out briefly. There can be water on the trail throughout this section any time of the year. The trail climbs a rock river and then bends left and crosses the creek again. After the crossing there is more storm damage. The Flat Peter Trail crosses Dismal Branch two more times and enters a flat area enclosed by a rhododendron tunnel. Here on the north side of Pine Swamp Ridge is the headwaters of Dismal Branch.

Just before a right bend, about 4.1 miles from the trailhead, there is a small clearing and a clear, flat campsite. The trail bends right and begins to climb to the saddle between Dismal Branch and Dixon Branch. The climb is more gradual than earlier and the rhododendron is left behind being replaced by thickets of laurel. At the saddle, 4.5 miles from the trailhead, there is a small wilderness sign. In the saddle, turning right and doing a short bushwhack of 0.4 miles leads to the top of Peters Mountain and the Allegheny Trail (See Allegheny Trail description).

From here, the trail descends to Dixon Branch and the trailhead on FS 722. This moderate descent begins in a huge fern field with the ferns waist high in places. The trail can be difficult to follow because of the ferns, so watch closely for the yellow blazes. The trail exits the fern fields through an opening in a rhododendron thicket and becomes easier to follow. A large tulip popular guards the entrance. After entering the rhododendron thicket, there is a campsite on the right. Right after the campsite, the trail makes the first of several creek crossings. None of the crossings are very difficult.

After 10 crossing, Dixon Branch ties into the North Fork. At this junction, the trail turns left and crosses Dixon Branch. There is a bridge to assist in the crossing. On the other side of the bridge is a large campsite and some old railroad wheels can be seen in the creek. These bridges are 6.9 miles from the trailhead. The trail turns right and crosses the North Fork. After this crossing, the trail begins to follow a clearly defined road which has not seen traffic in some time. At 7.6 miles the trail crosses Dixon Creek again. There is a bridge, however, this bridge is of the one log variety and bounces a great deal - so be careful.

After the crossing, the trail bends right and begins a short, steep climb followed by an equally steep descent back to the creek. At the creek the trail is again flat. There are many posted signs and a single strand of barbed wire on the left. The forest in this area is composed of hickory, maple, and oak. The trail follows the National Forest boundary for about 0.7 miles an dumps out onto FS 722. At the road, turn left and walk about 0.3 miles to the parking area.

A log in the process of being reclaimed by nature.

Ground Hog Trail   4

Length: 1.3 Miles
Time: 1 Hour
Difficulty: Moderate
Elevation Change: 1,200 Feet
USGS Maps: Interior
Trailhead: CR 635

How To Get There

Take I-81 to Exit #121. Follow US 460 West to Blacksburg. At the intersection of US 460 Bypass and US 460 Business just west of Blackburg, travel 16 miles to CR 635. Turn right on CR 635 and proceed 7.6 miles to a parking area on the left side of the road. There are two blue blazes on a telephone pole on the right side of the road.

Trail Description

This is a steep trail from Stony Creek to the crest of Peters Mountain and a junction with the Appalachain Trail. The trail, at times, follows old road grade and at other times it is a narrow footpath. The Groundhog Trail travels for a short time along a small creek, but for the most part it is dry. There is very little debris across the trail and it appears to be well maintained. The Groundhog Trail is marked with blue blazes.

The trail begins at a little parking area on the left side of the road. The climb is moderate at the beginning. After a bend to the left and the trail's grade becomes more difficult. There are many large hardwoods throughout this area. Some species include poplar, oak, and hickory. At 0.3 miles the trail makes a bend to the right and the grade is difficult. The trail crosses a small creek, and the creek is now on the left. The area starts to take on the look of a moist region as white pine and hemlock become more common. The creek is crossed again and the trail becomes almost flat. Use this respite well as the trail becomes quite steep again.

At 0.7 miles, the creek is left behind as the trail begins to climb rapidly toward the crest. Hardwoods again become the dominate species, and the trail finally begins to flatten out near the summit. The trail reaches the ridge top in Dickenson Gap. There is a good sized rock which is painted red and is a boundary marker for the National Forest. The trail connects with the AT in this gap. From this location, a right on the AT goes north, while a left heads to the south. Either way, there is a climb (See AT description).

The junction of the AT with the Allegheny Trail.

Forest Service Trail 268   5

Length: 0.60 Miles
Time: 15 Minutes
Elevation Change: 100 Feet
Difficulty: Easy
USGS Maps: Interior
Trailhead: Near the Cherokee Flats Parking Area

How To Get There

Via the AT or the Flat Peter Loop Trail

Trail Description

This trail is a short trail connecting the Appalachain Trail to the Flat Peter Loop Trail. Located outside the wilderness boundary, the trail is actually an old road. Since the trail parallels the lower end of Dismal Branch, the grade is easy. When the AT turns left and crosses Dismal Branch (See AT description), FS Trail P268 continues straight. After a short distance it crosses a small creek and enters a rhododendron tunnel. The trail crosses another small feeder creek and begins a very gradual climb. There is a wide trail junction where P268 connects with the Flat Peter Trail.

A right leads up Dismal Branch, while continuing straight leads to Kellys Flat. There is a great clearing along the trail through Kellys Flat. Once in the clearing, an immediate left leads into another large clearing. Continuing straight leads to the trailhead for the Flat Peter Loop Trail on FS 722 (See Flat Peter Loop Trail description).

Ramseys Draft Wilderness

Ramseys Draft

Ramseys Draft is located in the western part of Augusta County about twenty-two miles west of Staunton, Virginia. The wilderness, located in the George Washington National Forest, was created by Congress in 1984 and encompasses an area of approximately 6,500 acres.

The wilderness includes the eastern side of Shenandoah Mountain and western slope of the ridge leading up to Big Bald Knob. Included in the wilderness is the entire upper drainage for Ramseys Draft, a large creek with its headwaters near the top of Hardscrabble Knob. Hardscrabble Knob is the highest point in the Ramseys Draft area with an elevation of 4,282 feet. There are two other peaks over 4,000 feet in the wilderness, Big Bald Knob and Tearjacket Knob.

This roadless area has an extensive trail system with approximately twenty-nine miles of trails in and around the wilderness area. Most of the trails are well maintained, easy to hike, and cover an extensive area of the wilderness area. The Ramseys Draft Trail follows the Ramseys Draft, a clear flowing stream, to its headwaters. Another series of trails completely circumnavigate the primitive area. There are plenty of places to camp in the wilderness area and water is readily available. However, if hiking along the Shenandoah Trail, it is advisable to carry water.

The forest of the Ramseys Draft Wilderness is like no other forest in the state and quite possibly on the East Coast. This forest has been managed as a wild area since purchased by the government in 1916. The Ramseys Draft Wilderness contains one of the largest stands of virgin timber east of the Mississippi River. The trees are enormous, in fact, the largest hemlock in the state is located within the boundaries of the Ramseys Draft Wilderness. Ramseys Draft could probably be described as the wilderness of trees. On a sadder note, many of the hemlock are now being infected by a rust blight. The blight is killing many of the large hemlock and little can be done to stop its spread.

The most interesting aspect of the wilderness area is its trees. However, the trees are but one of many beautiful aspects in the wilderness. Hardscrabble Knob, the highest point in the wilderness, is a great place. At the top of Hardscrabble Knob is a set of rocks which lie above the trees. The view from this set of rocks is magnificent. Another interesting area is Freezelands Flats, a small bald located on the eastern shoulder on Shenandoah Mountain. Finally, there is a unique spot along the crest of the ridge running to the top of Big

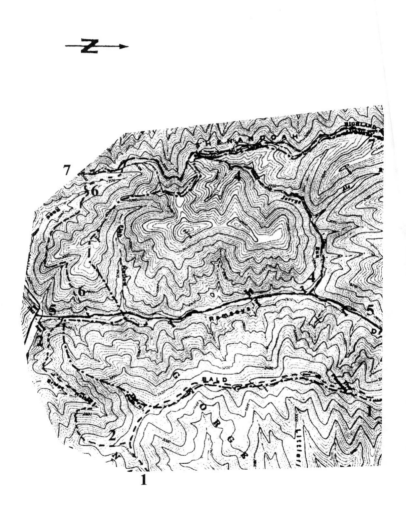

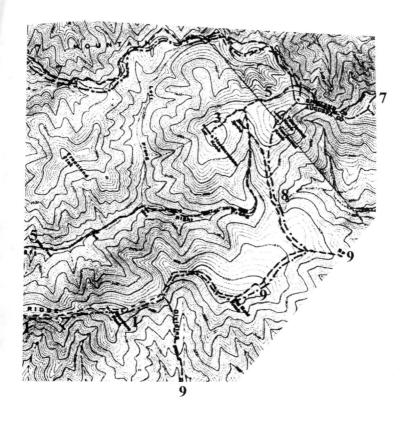

Bald Knob. Between The Peak and The Pinnacle, is a place where the big hemlocks march to the ridge top. The eastern slope is covered with chestnut oak. The two ecosystems come together at the ridge crest and provide a stark contrast between the drier eastern slope and the wetter more sheltered western slope.

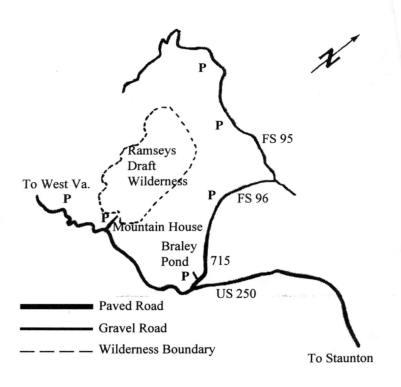

Bald Knob Trail 1

Length: 7.5 Miles (One Way)
Time: 4 Hours
Elevation Change: 1,900 Feet
Difficulty: Moderately Difficult
USGS Map: West Augusta
Trailhead: Braley Pond on FS 349-1

How To Get There

Take I-81 to Exit #225 just north of Staunton. Turn west on the Woodrow Wilson Parkway (Route 275), travel 5.5 miles to US 250. Turn west on US 250 and travel 14.5 miles to CR 715. Take a right on CR 715 and travel 0.3 miles to FS 349-1. Turn left on the FS road and travel 0.7 miles to the Braley Pond Picnic area.

Trail Description

The trail begins near the picnic area at Braleys Pond. There is an information center near a small bridge. Cross the bridge and climb the earthen dam, and at the top of the dam go to the right. The trail skirts the edge of the pond. On the back side of the pond there is a small bridge which crosses a shallow creek. There is a sign indicating the distance to the Wild Oak Trail (7 miles) and the Ramseys Draft Trail (11 miles). The Bald Knob Trail is marked with yellow blazes.

The trail begins on a gravel road and passes through three small clearings. Near the third clearing the creek forks, the trail crosses the creek, and follows the left fork. After a short distance this creek is forded again. About 150 feet beyond the creek crossing, the trail turns right off the road and begins an uphill climb. There are two yellow blazes to mark the trail junction with the road - be on the lookout for these blazes. The trail is well maintained and easy to follow. The grade is moderate and the forest is mainly mixed hardwoods with a few small pines.

The climb continues to be moderate. There are occasional glimpses of the surrounding valleys including one outstanding view of Western Augusta County. After a long gradual right bend, the trail enters a large bowl and then climbs to the top of a narrow shoulder. This finger ridge has a campsite and a commanding view to the east. The east side of the ridge is comprised of mainly hardwoods, while the west side is dominated by the pines.

The trail turns left and climbs out of the bowl. There are some nice views, but only from late fall to early spring. The trail swings right and enters a second smaller bowl. At the end of this bowl there is a small rock river and some very large red oak trees. The trail turns left and climbs out of the bowl. Near the ridge top is a red oak with a <u>very</u> large burl on the trunk. When the Bald Knob Trail reaches a large flat area, the junction with the Bridge Hollow Trail is near.

At 3.4 miles, the Bald Knob Trail intersects the Bridge Hollow Trail and the Bridge Hollow Trail exits to the left and heads downhill (See Bridge Hollow Trail description). The Bald Knob Trail continues to climb uphill. The trail traverses a small knob, then begins climbing to The Peak staying to the left of the summit. During this climb the trail enters the wilderness area and there is a small sign marking the boundary. The distance from The Peak to the trail junction is 0.3 miles. The trail descends and enters a long saddle with a good view to the east.

The footpath meanders through a flat area covered with oak, pine, and hemlock. This is an excellent spot for camping. Beyond is a rocky ridge top with a good view of Great North Mountain at 4,463 feet and smaller House Mountain in the distance. Next, there is a short, narrow, grassy ridge. This ridge presents a wonderful contrast of vegetation. The hemlock from the Draft march up the ridge from the west, while chestnut oak march up the ridge top from the east. These two distinct ecosystems come to together at the crest, and the contrast between the lush green western slope and the dry eastern slope is amazing.

The trail begins the climb toward the top of The Pinnacle, 3,841 feet. The distance from The Peak to The Pinnacle is 2 miles. The trail winds through a stand of stunted red oak and then enters a stand of tall hemlock. The trail stays to the left of The Pinnacle summit. Leaving The Pinnacle behind, there are two steep climbs before reaching Gordons Peak. Gordons Peak is the highest point on the Bald Knob Trail at 3,915 feet. The trail again misses the top traveling just west of the summit. The distance from The Pinnacle to Gordons Peak is 1.2 miles. Beyond Gordons Peak is an area of large oak and small laurel. There is a small set of rocks to climb, but the climb is not difficult.

The trail enters a clearing with a small pond. Here the Wild Oak Trail enters from the right. The distance from Gordons Peak to the junction with the Wild Oak Trail is 0.5 miles. The Bald Knob Trail ends; however, the hike can be continued on the Wild Oak Trail (See Wild Oak Trail description).

Bridge Hollow Trail   2

Length: 2 Miles (One Way)
Time: 1.5 Hours
Difficulty: Moderate
Elevation Change: 1,100 Feet
USGS Map: West Augusta
Trailhead: Mountain House Picnic Area

How To Get There

Via the Ramseys Draft Trail.

Trail Description

The Bridge Hollow Trail is a new trail which connects the Ramseys Draft Trail to the Bald Knob Trail. When joined with the Wild Oak Trail and the Tearjacket Trail, a long circuit hike through the Ramseys Draft Wilderness Area is created. This trail, approximately 2 miles in length climbs from 2,300 feet to 3,400 feet. The climb is slow and gradual with only a few places which could be characterized as steep and these sections are few and far between.

The Bridge Hollow Trail gets it name from the hollow which the trail traverses. To reach the beginning of the trail, hike approximately 100 yards up the Ramseys Draft Trail to where there is a small wooden sign marking the trail. The Bridge Hollow Trail exits the Ramseys Draft Trail to the right and immediately crosses the Draft. There is a small log bridge with a railing for support. Just beyond the bridge is a small campsite. The trail begins with a short steep climb out of the Draft. Large hemlocks are left behind almost immediately and are replaced by large chestnut oak, red oak, white pine, and mountain laurel.

When the trail makes a hard left turn it enters Bridge Hollow. Once in the hollow, the path travels around the hollow to the opposite side and joins with the Bald Knob Trail. In this hollow, there are many large oak trees. The junction is in a large flat area on the shoulder of the Peak. The Bridge Hollow Trail ends at the junction. A right on the Bald Knob Trail leads to Braleys Pond and a left leads to the Wild Oak Trail (See Bald Knob Trail description).

Hardscrabble Knob Trail 3

Length: 0.4 miles
Time: 30 Minutes
Difficulty: Easy
Elevation Change: 250 Feet
USGS Map: West Augusta
Trailhead: Via the Ramseys Draft Trail

How To Get There

Via The Ramseys Draft Trail

Trail Description

The Hardscrabble Knob Trail is a short, easy climb from the saddle between Hardscrabble Knob and Tearjacket Knob to the top of Hardscrabble Knob. The trail begins at a elevation of 4,050 feet and climbs to an elevation of 4,282 feet at the summit of the knob. This is the highest point in the Ramseys Draft Wilderness Area. This short trail is worth the effort as the view from the rocky summit is superb.

The trail begins at the junction of the Ramseys Draft Trail and the Hardscrabble Knob Trail after a 5.5 mile hike up the Ramseys Draft (See Ramseys Draft Trail description). A small sign marks the beginning of the trail which exits to the left, and winds its way through a mixture of hardwoods and pines. At the summit there is an old wooden structure and the remains of an old fire tower, which is lying on its side. The tower whispers the question to all who have ever climbed one: "What will I do if this thing falls?"

The tower is located near a large pile of rock and the top of this rock pile is above the trees. From this vantage point, the view of the surrounding area is wonderful. Several peaks are visible to the south including Crawford Mountain, Great North Mountain, House Mountain, Sharp Top and Flat Top. These last two peaks are located at Peaks of Otter. There is also a great view into the heart of the Ramseys Draft area.

Jerrys Run Trail 4

Length: 2 Miles (One Way)
Time: 1.5 Hours
Difficulty: Moderate
Elevation Change: 700 Feet
USGS Map: West Augusta
Trailhead: Via the Ramseys Draft Trail

How To Get There

Via the Ramseys Draft Trail or the Shenandoah Mountain Trail.

Trail Description

The Jerrys Run Trail is a short two mile trail which ties together Ramseys Draft Trail and the Shenandoah Mountain Trail. The trail travels along Jerrys Run, a small creek that drains into Ramseys Draft. The Jerrys Run Trail is a condensed version of the Ramseys Draft Trail and the scenery along this small creek is beautiful. Towering hemlock, white pine, and oak dominate the landscape. Add to this a small, clear creek and you have one of the best short hikes in the state. The trail is not extremely difficult climbing from 2,500 feet at the Draft to 3,200 feet on the ridge top.

Jerrys Run Trail is located approximately 1.5 miles from the Ramseys Draft trailhead at the Mountain House Picnic Area (See Ramseys Draft Trail description). The trail starts just after crossing Jerrys Run on the Ramseys Draft Trail. Just before the trail junction is a deep ford created by Jerrys Run. Beyond the ford is a small sign marking the trailhead which exits to the left and enters a narrow valley with steep walls. Moving in a westerly direction away from Ramseys Draft, the huge hemlock and white pine gives one a true perspective of our size in the world.

The trail fords Jerrys Run four times before reaching the junction with Als Run. Als Run enters Jerrys Run from the right. The trail meanders up the left creek which is Jerrys Run. Until now Jerrys Run Trail has been a gradual climb. Once past the junction with Als Run, the trail begins climbing to the top of Shenandoah Mountain. Although never real steep, the climb is continous.

Near the end of the climb, the creek veers to the right away from the trail. When the creek is left behind, the moisture which the creek provided disappears as do the large hemlocks. The trail's appearance changes dramatically over the last .3 miles as the hemlocks are replaced by the large oak and hickory.

The Jerrys Run Trail terminates at the junction with the Shenandoah Mountain Trail. At this junction, a right leads to the Ramseys Draft Trail. A left leads to the Road Hollow Trail or the parking area at the top of Shenandoah Mountain (See Shenandoah Mountain Trail description).

168

Ramseys Draft Trail   5

Length: 7 Miles (One Way)
Time: 4 Hours
Elevation Change: 1,500 Feet
Difficulty: Moderately Difficult
USGS Map: West Augusta, Palo Alto
Trailhead: Route 250, Mountain House Picnic Area

How To Get There

Take I-81 to Exit #225 north of Staunton. Turn west on the Woodrow Wilson Parkway (Route 275). Travel 5.5 miles to US 250. Turn west on US 250 and travel 19.8 miles to the entrance of the Mountain House Picnic Area. Turn left into the picnic area, cross a low water bridge and proceed 0.1 miles to the parking area and trailhead.

Trail Description

Hiking in the Ramseys Draft is truly an experience of immense proportions. The trail contains some of the largest white pine and hemlock found in the State of Virginia. The crowns of these trees form a canopy far overhead creating what could truly be called a Cathedral to Nature. However, it is not just the evergreens which are immense. Many hardwoods such as tulip poplar and oak have also been left to the whims of nature and not just the whims of man. In this area one might actually see a snag which died of old age.

The trail is long and if hiking the whole length, pack a lunch and plan on spending the entire day. The trail follows an old road bed and the grade is easy for the first 4.3 miles. Once the road bed is left behind the trail is steeper; however, the grade is still very manageable. This section of trail is approximately two miles long.

The major problem with the Ramseys Draft Trail are the severe washouts which occurred in 1969 and again in 1985. These washouts have made the trail non-existent in some places. The Draft must be crossed many times and the crossings can be difficult especially if the creek is running high. However, the floods have washed down many trees which criss-cross the creek. These "natural" log bridges can be used on many occasions for easy crossing.

The trail begins at the Mountain House Picnic Area and passes a Forest Service information and sign-in center. About 0.25 miles beyond the information center, the Bald Knob Trail exits to the right and then the Road Hollow Trail exits to the left. The next section of the trail has been washed out but skirts the left creek bank and the rocks along side the creek. This is a very difficult section in high water. Beyond this area, the trail becomes an old road bed passing by an old Forest Service building on the right. The trail continues along the left side of the creek and is lined by many large hemlocks.

A Ramseys Draft Wilderness sign, on the left side of the trail, is located just before the first ford of the Draft. This first ford has a large log jam and the log jam can be used to cross the creek. If utilizing the jam be aware that there are sections with loose debris and a twisted ankle is not out of the realm of possibility. On the other side of the creek is a very large black birch. About half way to the second ford there is a large hole in the trail. The second ford can be crossed on a log jam but pick the way carefully.

The third ford of the creek can be accomplished on a single log which crosses the creek. Beyond this third ford, the trail becomes indistinct and hard to follow. Orange blazes have been used to mark the trail. The creek separates into many small streams and there are several smaller fords to cross before reaching the right side of the creek. Once on the right side of the creek, the road becomes the trail again.

The next ford can be done on a log. Just before the ford there are remains of old wire cages once used to prevent erosion. After the ford the road reappears and the creek is on the left. Throughout this area are large, beautiful pines and the trail becomes hard to follow. There is another series of orange blazes which serve as a guide. The creek is forded again, and the crossing is easy when the water is low. However, if the water is high there is an old tree which can be utilized as a one log bridge. Beyond the ford the road reappears on the right side of the creek.

The next crossing is at Jerrys Run which can be recognized by the short steep drop to a small creek followed a short steep climb up the other side. The creek crossing is not difficult unless the water is high. If the water is up continue up Jerrys Run to find an easier ford. Once on the other side of Jerrys Run, there is an oak tree at the point where Jerrys Run and the Ramseys Draft come together. This tree is unusual because beautiful ferns grow up the trunk. At 2.3 miles, there is a sign marking the junction of Jerrys Run Trail. Jerrys Run Trail exits to the left (See Jerrys Run Trail description).

Not far beyond the sign, the creek is forded again. The trail is hard to follow and orange blazes serve as a guide. In this area, are many small pools of water, the bottoms of which are covered with small rocks and pebbles. The creek is forded again and is now on the right. After the ford there is a pleasant stroll through a laurel thicket. Beyond the thicket is another ford at an old concrete bridge abutment. After the crossing the grade becomes steeper, but only for a short distance. In this area hardwoods are the dominant species, and there is a campsite on the right near an old culvert.

The Ramseys Draft

The Draft is forded again and another small feeder creek is crossed, just beyond this creek is a hemlock with a 13 foot circumference. After two more fords there is an open area and the road ends. The clearing is 2 miles from the Jerrys Run trailhead. Here, Ramseys Draft splits into the Left Prong and the Right Prong. The Draft Trail continues up the Right Prong. There is a campsite in this open area and plenty of water to drink, however, remember to treat the water. There was a USGS marker placed near here in 1964. The elevation is 2,914 feet.

Now the road is left behind and the trail begins to climb. The first obstacle to tackle is a large hemlock across the trail. Just beyond the hemlock is a red oak with a circumference of ten feet. The creek is forded again, and a hemlock with a circumference of fifteen feet is visible.

The next area is truly spectacular. There is a large open area surrounded by huge hemlocks, and the canopy formed by these tall trees is high overhead. There is a campsite on the other side of the creek. To top it off, there are some great pools of water deep enough to sit in and relax.

After another small ford is a large rock slide, and the water can be heard rushing under the rocks. This area provides a glimpse of how the ancient forests in the state might have once looked. There are several large hemlocks lying across the trail and a small campsite by the creek. There is another small ford and the valley becomes very narrow with steep walls. The trail moves up the left side of this narrow valley. This area marks the transition from the wet sheltered area of the Draft to the drier more exposed areas of the ridge top. The hemlock slowly gives way to the birch, oak, and hickory.

The Ramseys Draft Trail joins the Tearjacket Trail 1.9 miles from the USGS benchmark. The tearjacket Trail exits to the right, and at the junction there is a sign stating Bald Knob (See Tearjacket Trail description). Hiner Spring is located on the left in a small protected area. The region is very flat and very wet. A short hike of 0.25 miles leads to the junction with the Hardscrabble Knob Trail. This trail exits the Ramseys Draft Trail to the left, and leads to the highest point in the Ramseys Draft Wilderness (See Hardscrabble Knob Trail description). There are many campsites located in the area between Hiner Spring and the Hardscrabble Knob Trail.

The Ramseys Draft Trail begins a slight descent at the Hardscrabble Knob Trail junction. It traverses two small hollows before entering an area of very large oak. At 0.7 miles from the junction with the Hardscrabble Knob Trail, the Ramseys Draft Trail joins the Shenandoah Mountain Trail. A right leads north out of the wilderness area and a left leads south to the Jerrys Run Trail and the Road Hollow Trail (See Shenandoah Mountain Trail description).

Road Hollow Trail   6

Lenght: 2 Miles (One Way)
Time: 1.5 Hours
Difficulty: Moderately Difficult
Elevation Change: 600 Feet
USGS Maps: West Augusta
Trailhead: Via the Ramseys Draft Trail

How To Get There

Via the Ramseys Draft Trail and the Shenandoah Mountain Trail.

Trail Description

The Road Hollow Trail is a connector trail for the Ramseys Draft Trail and the Shenandoah Mountain Trail. The trail, which is 2 miles long, is well laid out but is not located within the wilderness. There is an easy climb from the Draft Trail to the top of the ridge. The elevation change is only about 600 feet; therefore, this trail provides easy access to the top of Shenandoah Mountain. The only major drawback is the noise from cars and trucks as they make their way up to the top of the mountain.

To reach the Road Hollow Trail, begin at the Ramseys Draft trailhead. About 0.25 miles beyond the Forest Service information center is the trail jucntion. The trail exits left and begins with a short, steep climb away from the Ramseys Draft. Along the way the trail passes under many large hemlock and white pine. After a right bend the trail enters the first of two hollows. In the first hollow is a mix of pine, hemlock and hardwoods. The trail drops slightly just before crossing a small stream. Beyond the creek the trail begins to climb again and bends right entering a second hollow.

This area has a mix of hardwoods such as chestnut oak, white oak, red oak, hickory, and maple. The trail contours up the right side of the hollow and leaves the sounds of the world behind. After traversing the second hollow, the Road Hollow Trail makes its final climb to the top. At the top of the ridge the Road Hollow Trail joins the Shenandoah Mountain Trail. A short trip to the south leads to the

the Shenandoah Mountain trailhead. Turning right leads to the Jerrys Run Trail and the Ramseys Draft Trail (See Shenandoah Mountain Trail description).

A snow shelf on a ridge crest near The Pinnacle.

Shenandoah Mountain Trail 7

Length: 10.8 Miles (One Way)
Time: 5 Hours
Difficulty: Moderate
Elevation Change: 1,100 Feet
USGS Maps: Mcdowell, West Augusta
Trailheads: US. 250, FS 95

<u>How to Get There</u>

Southern Trailhead--Take I-81 to Exit #225 north of Staunton. Turn west on the Woodrow Wilson Parkway (Route 275). Travel 5.5 miles to US 250. Turn west on US 250 and travel 21.8 to the top of Shenandoah Mountain. The parking area and trailhead are on the right.

Northern Trailhead--Take I-81 to Exit #225 north of Staunton. Turn west on the Woodrow Wilson Parkway (Route 275). Travel 5.5 miles to US 250. Turn west on US 250 and travel 14.5 miles to CR 715. Turn right on CR 715 and proceed 5.8 miles to the stop sign. At the "T" intersection, take a left on FS 95 and travel 6.0

miles to the top of Shenandoah Mountain. Parking and the trailhead are on the left.

Trail Description

The Shenandoah Mountain Trail winds its way across the top of Shenandoah Mountain, and is an excellent mountain trail because of its easy grade. Unlike many trails throughout the mountains of Virginia, the Shenandoah Mountain Trail begins high on the mountain, approximately 2,900 feet, and slowly climbs to about 4,100 feet near the junction with the Ramseys Draft Trail. The trail is a series of long gradual climbs followed by shallow dips. The Shenandoah Mountain Trail skirts the western edge of Ramseys Draft. However, it is an integral part of the trail system for the Ramseys Draft Wilderness. This trail description begins at the northern end of the trail and terminates at the southern end of the trail.

The trail begins on the left side of FS 95 near a small sign with yellow blazes. The moderate grade is fairly consistant throughout the first section of the trail. The trail is easy to follow and well maintained. At just under 0.5 miles is a blaze and just past this blaze, the trail makes a left turn.

The forest understory becomes thick and crowds the sides of the trail with mountain laurel dominating the understory. At approximately 1.5 miles the trail tops the ridge and the forest opens up. The climb to this point has been kind and gentle.

For the next mile the path contours the mountainside with perhaps a slight incline. Once the trail tops the ridge it leads slightly to the left side of the crest and after a short distance passes back over the ridge top to the right side of the crest. Throughout this region, there is evidence of a very harsh environment. There is a great deal of downed timber, and the standing trees are knotted and gnarled. Snow may remain on some of these ridges into April.

At approximately 2.5 miles, the grade increases slightly but the grade remains moderate. When high mountain hemlock dot the landscape, watch for the wilderness boundary sign. The sign is about 3.0 miles from FS 95. The junction with the Ramseys Draft Trail is at 3.6 miles. The Ramseys Draft Trail exits to the left (See Ramseys Draft Trail description). At the junction with the Ramseys Draft Trail, approximately 3,900 feet, the Shenandoah Mountain Trail continues in a southerly direction on the western side of the mountain. The region is heavily wooded with pine and chestnut oak, while mountain laurel makes up much of the growth in the understory.

In a small saddle 0.6 miles from the Ramseys Draft Trail junction is the junction with the Sinclair Hollow Trail. In this saddle there are large red oak, white pine, and hemlock. The Sinclair Hollow Trail exits to the right beginning a steep decent to the Shaw's Fork Road about 2 miles below. The Shenandoah Mountain Trail goes left into the Ramseys Draft watershed entering a small saddle The trail continues to meander in and out of the wilderness area for the next three miles with good views of both the western mountains as well as the Ramseys Draft. The trail begins a long contour of a major bowl on the west side of the mountain before entering a saddle with steep drops on both sides. The saddle is home to a beautiful stand of hemlock.

The trail continues to contour the mountain to the junction with Jerrys Run Trail. This junction is 4.2 miles from the junction with the Sinclair Hollow Trail. The Jerrys Run Trail exits to the left (See Jerrys Run Trail description). The Shenandoah Mountain Trail continues its southward journey leaving the Ramseys Draft Wilderness area just beyond the Jerrys Run Trail. The trail sweeps around another large bowl before connecting with the Road Hollow Trail. This trail exits to the left (See Road Hollow Trail description). The junction with the Road Hollow Trail is about 1.2 miles from the junction with Jerrys Run Trail.

Beyond the Road Hollow Trail, the Shenandoah Mountain Trail continues on to its end at the parking area on US 250. The trailhead for the Shenandoah Mountain Trail is 1.2 miles from the junction with the Road Hollow Trail. At the southern trailhead ther is a parking area with historical information about Confederate breastworks built in the early part of the Civil War.

Tearjacket Trail   8

Length: 1.2 Miles
Time: 45 Minutes
Elevation Change: 100 Feet
Difficulty: Easy To Moderate
USGS Map: West Augusta
Trailhead: Via Wild Oak Trail or Ramseys Draft Trail

<u>How To Get There</u>

Via the Wild Oak Trail and the Ramseys Draft Trail

Trail Description

The Tearjacket Trail, tying together the Wild Oak Trail and the Ramseys Draft Trail, is very easy with only one small climb. Although called the Tearjacket Trail, the trail does not climb to the summit of Tearjacket Knob, the second highest point in the Ramseys Draft Wilderness Area at 4,229 feet.

To reach the Tearjacket Trail, hike up either the Ramseys Draft Trail (See Ramseys Draft Trail description) or the Wild Oak Trail (See Wild Oak Trail description). This trail description begins at the junction with the Wild Oak Trail and proceeds to the junction with the Ramseys Draft Trail. The Tearjacket Trail exits the Wild Oak Trail at the "Y" 1.5 miles from the trailhead at Camp Todd. At the trail junction of the Wild Oak Trail and the Tearjacket Trail, there is a small sign marking the trail. The trail has an easy grade traveling through a mix of hardwoods with occasional pines and hemlocks. Near the junction, there are many large boulders scattered through the forest. There is an old wire strung through the trees and some of the trees have old electrical insulators nailed to them.

After meandering through a flat region the trail begins its only serious climb, and although short, it is fairly steep. In this vicinity there is a laurel thicket which the trail weaves through. Beyond the thicket the Tearjacket Trail descends to the headwaters of the Ramseys Draft. At the junction with the Ramseys Draft Trail is a sign marking the direction to Bald Knob. Just to the left of this trail junction is Hiner Spring. A right on the Ramseys Draft Trail leads to the the Hardscrabble Knob Trail and the Shenandoah Mountain Trail, while a left leads to the trailhead for the Ramseys Draft Trail (See Ramseys Draft Trail description).

Wild Oak Trail   9

Length: 5.25 Miles (One Way)
Time: 3 Hours
Difficulty: Difficult
Elevation Change: 1520 Feet
USGS Map: West Augusta
Trailhead: FS 96 and FS 95
How To Get There

Take I-81 to Exit #225 north of Staunton. Turn west on the Woodrow Wilson Parkway (Route 275). Travel 5.5 miles to US

250. Turn west on US 250 and travel 14.5 miles to CR 715. Turn right on CR 715 and travel 4.2 miles to the large sign announcing the Wild Oak Trail. CR 715 changes to FS 95. There is parking on the left.

A second trailhead is located on FS 95. Continue on FS 96 to the stop sign approximately 5.8 miles from US 250. At the "T" intersection, take a left on FS 95 and travel 3.0 miles to the Camp Todd sign. Parking and the trailhead are on the left.

Trail Description

The Wild Oak Trail is another trail which can be utilized to gain access to the Ramseys Draft Wilderness. This trail begins on FS 96 and ends on FS 95 and utilizing the two FS roads makes for a nice circuit hike. The trail is also an integral part of the Draft trail system creating a link between the lower Draft and the upper Draft areas. The Wild Oak Trail, from FS 96 to its intersection with the Bald Knob Trail, is a trail with a single purpose: To get to the top of the ridge. Although difficult, the trail is pleasant and rewards the hiker with a rest by a high mountain pond at nearly 3,800 ft.

The trail begins at a parking lot on the left side of FS 96, with a sign marking the trailhead. White blazes mark the trail and are helpful, especially at the fork within the first 0.5 miles of the trail. At this fork take a left. Travel becomes more difficult as the first steep section is encountered. This section is short and is followed by a camping area near the trail. Water is available in the nearby stream.

About 100 yards after passing the campsite there is a large dirt mound in the center of the trail. This mound is an excellent landmark for a small waterfall that lies to the right. To get a good view of this fall, cross over the dirt mound, take a right off the trail, and head down to the stream. Be careful - the canyon walls are steep.

After the waterfall the trail again becomes steep and remains steep to the crest of the ridge. There is another short level section at about 2.0 miles with a campsite to the left. From this point, except for a switchback to skirt a boulder, the trail travels virtually straight up the ridge.

At 2.5 miles the trail reaches the crest of the ridge. A sign gives directions to Bald Knob (a right). The Bald Knob Trail joins the Wild Oak Trail from the left. A left leads to the Braley Pond Picnic Area and the Bridge Hollow Trail (See Bald Knob Trail description). The small pond at this intersection is a great place to rest and contemplate the climb up the ridge. From this point everything to

Virgin hemlock stand along the Ramseys Draft.

the west is wilderness land. The Wild Oak Trail, traveling along the ridge top to the intersection with Tearjacket Trail creates part of the eastern boundary of the area.

Beyond the junction with the Bald Knob Trail, there is a steep climb to a region littered with windfall. Just past the windfall is another steep climb which leads to a beautiful flat spot covered with laurel thickets. The trail passes through the thickets eventually leading to a small clearing on the summit of the Big Bald Knob, eleva-

179

tion 4,125 feet. The distance from the trail junction to the top of the bald is 0.9 miles. The area is covered with small oak, maple, hemlock, and pine.

After leaving the clearing the trail begins a long, gradual descent to the Tearjacket Trail. Be on the lookout for a small open area on the right because the view from this small opening is exceptional. There are unobstructed views of both the Shenandoah National Park and Massanutten Mountain. The Tearjacket Trail exits to the left and forms a "Y" at the intersection (See Tearjacket Trail Description). The distance from the top of the bald to the trail junction is 0.7 miles.

After the trail junction, Wild Oak Trail exits the Ramseys Draft Wilderness and descends to the FS 96. This area is flat and dominated by hemlock and white pine. At a springhead near the trail the grade becomes moderate. Just beyond the springhead, the trail begins a rapid descent and there is a good view to the east. Two switchbacks, one to the right and one to the left, mark the beginning of the descent.

The trail curves to the left and cuts through some rocks. The grade becomes more moderate. However, it does not last long as a switchback to the left signals the final drop to FS 96. There are many tall trees including some very large maples and a small creek on the right. The trail reaches FS 96, 1.3 miles from the junction with the Tearjacket Trail. There are several campsites at the bottom surrounded by tall white pine and maple. This area is called Camp Todd which was an old homesite for early settlers.

Rich
Hole
Wilderness

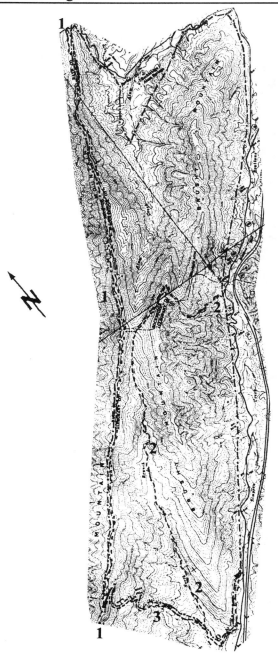

Rich Hole

The Rich Hole Wilderness is a small wilderness located in Rockbridge and Alleghany Counties about twelve miles west of Lexington, Virginia. The wilderness includes approximately 6500 acres in the James River District of the George Washington National Forest. The primitive area was created by Congress in 1987.

Rich Hole includes the upper drainage of Alum Springs which drains the northern portion of the wilderness. Simpson Creek drains the southeastern section and North Branch drains the southern end of the wilderness and flows almost totally within the wilderness boundary. The crest of Pleasant Mill Ridge is the western boundary and the eastern slope of Brushy Mountain forms the eastern boundary of the wilderness.

The wilderness has only one maintained trail, the Rich Hole Trail. White Rocks Tower Trail, located just south of the wilderness, forms the southern bounadary of the wilderness area. This road at one time led to a fire tower which stood at the top of the ridge. The only other area to hike is along Pleasant Mill Ridge. In all, the Rich Hole provides approximately eight miles of maintained trails and eleven miles of easy bushwhacking.

The major forest ecosystem of the Rich Hole is an oak-hickory forest. There are some very large specimens of oak trees along the White Rocks Tower Trail. In the sheltered cove of the upper reaches of Alum Springs, grow large hemlock and white pine. The ridge tops are dominated by chestnut oak and Virginia pine. There are also large thickets of rhododendron and mountain laurel located throughout the wilderness.

There are several interesting sites throughout the primitive area. First, along North Branch, iron mining used to be a viable activity and there are many signs of this prior activty. The second interesting area of the Rich Hole are the rocky outcrops on the eastern slope of Brushy Mountain. These rock outcrops run almost the entire length of the mountain. They are located across the top of the ridge as well as midway down the ridge. One of these outcrops, which can been seen from the Interstate 64, is quite large and has a rock column A third interesting aspect of the wilderness is the location of the spring head for North Branch. This spring flows right out of the middle of the Rich Hole Trail. Finally, there is the Potato Patch, an old farming homestead located about 0.75 miles from the beginning of the upper trailhead for the Rich Hole Trail.

The Rich Hole is blessed with many different animals, including game animals, and is a favorite hunting spot for many local area hunters. Therefore, it is best to avoid this area during hunting season.

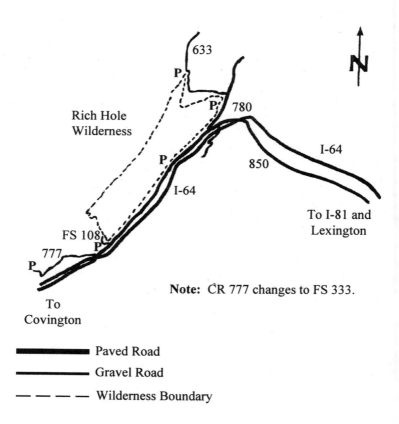

Note: CR 777 changes to FS 333.

━━━━━ Paved Road

─────── Gravel Road

─ ─ ─ ─ Wilderness Boundary

Pleasant Mill Ridge Trail/Bushwhack   1

Length: 10.5 miles (One Way)
Time: 6 Hours
Difficulty: Difficult
Elevation Change: 1,700 Feet
USGS Maps: Millboro, Nimrod Hall, Longdale Furnace
Trailhead: FS333 and CR 633

How To Get There

Northern Trailhead—Take I-81 to I-64 West, Exit #191, at Lexington. Take I-64 to Exit #43 and turn right at the stop sign. Travel 0.3 miles and turn right at the stop sign. Turn left on CR 850 and travel 0.8 miles. Turn right on to CR 780. Proceed 1.7 miles to CR 633 and turn left. Proceed 3.1 miles to a parking area on the left. This parking area is located at the Rockbridge\Bath County lines.

From Roanoke take US 220 to Clifton Forge. Take I-64 East to Exit #43 and turn left. Then follow the above directions.

Southern Trailhead—I-81 to I-64 West, Exit #191, at Lexington. Take I-64 to Exit #37 and turn east on CR 850. Travel 0.1 miles and turn left on to CR 777. After 0.6 miles, this road becomes FS 333. Travel 3.2 miles to the turn around. The trailhead is on the right.

From Roanoke take US 220 to Clifton Forge. Take I-64 East to Exit #37 and turn left. Then follow the above directions.

Trail Description

Pleasant Mill Ridge is located on the Rockbridge and Bath County lines. The Pleasant Mill Trail is not a maintained trail and unlike the Rich Hole Trail, does not have a clear path to follow. However, a journey along the ridge top makes for a great day hike. The trail is basically a series of game and hunter trails. It is relatively level with major climbs or descents located at either end of the trail. At the northern end of the trail, the elevation is approximately 2,100 feet. At the southern end of the trail the elevation is approximately 1,500 feet. The highest point on Pleasant Mill Ridge is approximately 3,200 feet. This trail begins at the trailhead located on CR 633 and ends at the parking area on FS 333. The direction of the trail is generally southward. One note of caution about this trail: There is no water along the route so pack plenty to drink.

There is no sign marking the parking area, but the trail begins by crossing a gate and taking the left fork toward the ridge top. Cross the first of three open meadows; this meadow is the home to many ferns. The second open area is dominated by a beautiful chinese chestnut. Near the third open area, there are many small chestnut trees. These small blight infected trees line the road/trail. The third clearing is dominated by a large red oak. Upon entering the third clearing, walk to the left past muscadine grape vines and sassafras trees. The road ends in this clearing but the trail continues on up into the woods near a large windfall.

The trail runs along a ridge top dominated by small chestnut oak, white pine, and Virginia pine. Along the crest are many dead Virginia pine, casualties of the Southern Pine Bark Beetle. Not too far beyond the last clearing is a three forked red oak with a flat rock embedded into the trunk. This rock makes a nice spot to rest weary legs and have a snack.

The ridge top narrows, becomes quite rocky, and leads to an abrupt drop. It is best to go down on the left side of the rocks. Once down, the trail enters an area of large oak and hickory trees. These trees create a park like setting and there are many signs of animal life in this region. This area gradually gives way to another rocky ridge top which offers a view of Brushy Mountain on the left and the Rough Mountain Wilderness on the right.

The trail enters another park like setting dominated by a very large black oak. This area again gives way to a rocky ridge with some very large stones and good views of Brushy Mountain and the Alum Springs Valley. When Brushy Mountain, on the left, reaches its highest elevation, one can turn left and do a short bushwhack of 0.5 miles across the saddle between Pleasant Mill Ridge and Brushy Mountain. This bushwhack leads to the Rich Hole Trail (See Rich Hole Trail description).

Continuing in a southwesterly direction along the ridge, leads to the remains of an old Forest Service fire tower built during the depression by the Civilian Conservation Corp. The White Rocks Tower Trail exits to the left (See White Rocks Tower Trail description). This junction also marks the southern boundary of the wilderness area. There is now an actual trail along the crest of Pleasant Mill Ridge. About 0.5 miles after the junction the trail makes a short, steep drop. Just beyond this drop, there is a large cliff on the left. A climb to the top of this cliff is well worth the effort as the view is truly outstanding. Rough Mountain Wilderness and Griffith Knob· can be seen to the west, while North Mountain and Brushy Mountain are to the east. The trail continues a gradual descent to FS 333. However, there is one more short, steep descent just before reaching the FS 333.

The Rich Hole Trail

Rich Hole Trail   2

Length: 6.0 miles
Time: 3.5 Hours
Difficulty: Moderate
Elevation Change: 1,920 Feet
USGS Maps: Longdale Furnace, Nimrod Hall
TrailHeads: FS 108 and Route 850

How To Get There

Take I-81 to I-64 West, Exit #191, at Lexington. Take I-64 to Exit #43. Turn right at the stop sign. Travel 0.3 miles and turn left onto CR 850. Travel 2.6 miles to the Rich Hole parking area. The parking area is on the right. This parking area is just beyond the top of the gap.

From Roanoke take US 220 to Clifton Forge. Take I-64 East to Exit #43 and turn left. Then follow the above directions.

To reach the lower parking area, travel past Exit #43. Take I-64 to Exit #37 and turn east on CR 850. Travel 1.3 miles to FS 108 and turn left. FS 108 is just beyond a small bridge. Travel 1.3 miles to a parking area on the left. There will be signs for the Rich Hole Wilderness and the White Rock Tower Trail. There is a gate at the beginning of FS 108 that may be closed. If it is closed, park and hike the 1.3 miles to the trailhead.

From Roanoke take US 220 to Clifton Forge. Take I-64 East to Exit #37 and turn left. Then follow the above directions.

Trail Description

The Rich Hole trail follows North Branch up between Pleasant Mill Ridge and Brushy Mountain. The trail crosses North Branch on thirteen occasions as it slowly climbs up the narrow hollow. The trail is approximately six miles long with an easy grade before making a rapid decent to the Rich Hole and the parking area on SR 850.

The trailhead is located near a small parking area on FS 108. A sign marks the boundary of the Rich Hole Wilderness and the beginning of the Rich Hole Trail. The trail begins in a deciduous forest comprised mainly of oak, poplar, and hickory. At 0.1 miles, the trail crosses a small brook, and there is Forest Service information center on the left. Beyond the information center, the trail begins in earnest. The first task is to ford the North Branch. This is an easy task in the summer when the weather has been dry, but in the spring expect to cross the creek with your boots off and your pants rolled up to your knees. On the other side of the creek, there is some large rhododendron and small mountain laurel.

At about 0.75 miles, there is a small cascade on the right. Just past the cascade, the trail crosses North Branch and then after approximately 100 yards the creek is forded again. After crossing a small feeder creek, the trail looks more like a path. The quality of the trail is still excellent. After the next ford, the creek will be on the left and the trail becomes a little fuzzy. When approaching the creek, it appears that there is another crossing which leads leads to a large windfall. Rather than fight the windfall, continue along the right side of the of the creek past the windfall. The trail is easy to pick up again and the grade remains easy.

The next section of trail affords some fine views of cliffs and rocks especially in the winter and early spring. Included in these vistas is a large rock overhang on the left just before a steep drop down to North Fork and another creek crossing. After the next crossing, there is a small water slide down a smooth rock face.

After this ford, the valley narrows considerably with many rocks and small cliffs on the left. Just past the rocks the creek must be forded again and the valley opens up. The trail continues along the creek passing some large poplar and red oak. At the next ford, there is a large black cherry and a beautiful stand of hemlock. There is a spot for camping under the hemlock trees. The creek starts to lose its strength and begins to disappear all together at times. Eventually, the main spring for the creek flows out of the ground almost in the middle of the trail. This area is approximately 3.2 miles from the trailhead.

Once past the spring the trail grade becomes more moderate and the Rich Hole Trail begins to climb up the right side of the valley. It passes through tangled thickets of rhododendron and mountain laurel. Following a slight descent, the trail enters the saddle between Alum Springs and the North Fork. A left across the saddle leads to the western boundary of the wilderness (See Pleasant Mill Ridge Trail description). A northward decent from the saddle leads into the Alum Spring drainage area - a tough bushwhack in its own right. There are no marked trails in this region, but the area is beautiful. The Alum Spring leads to the Rockbridge Alum Springs Resort which is privately owned. This small gap is at 4.1 miles. After the saddle, the land becomes drier and subsequently, there is a change in the forest ecosystem. The ridge is dominated by Virginia pine and chestnut oak. Many of these trees are very small. At the trail crest, about 4.7 miles from the the FS road, there is an old unreadable sign. From this location, one can bushwhack south by climbing to the top of Brushy Mountain and then follow the ridge back down to FS 108.

The trail begins to steeply descend to SR 850 and passes through an old field which has been overtaken by black locust. The Rich Hole Trail continues down passing through an old windfall which has been cleared of brush. Just beyond the windfall is a short trail to the right leading to the Potato Patch where old orchard trees still grow. The headwaters of Simpson Creek are also located in this region. About 5.3 miles from the trailhead, there is a rock overlook on the right. The view of North Mountain is very pleasant, but is marred by the sight of the I-64 and the power lines. At this point the trail begins to show signs of heavy use. Finally, the sounds of the interstate begin to invade the soft sound of the forest, and the realities of the world begin to interfere with the serenity of natural world. After crossing a small stream, there is a Forest Service information center is on the left. The trail ends at the upper parking area on SR 850.

White Rocks Tower Trail   3

Length: 1.5 miles
Time: 2.5 hours
Difficulty: Moderate
Elevation Change: 1,600 Feet
USGS Maps: Longdale Furnace, Nimrod Hall, Millboro,
Collierstown
Trailhead: FS 108

How To Get There

Take I-81 to I-64 West, Exit #191, at Lexington. Take I-64 to Exit #37. At the stop sign turn east on CR 850. Travel 1.3 miles to FS 108. Turn left on FS 108. This is a dirt road. The turn is just beyond a small bridge. Travel 1.3 miles to a parking area on the left. There is a sign marking the trail. There is a gate at the beginning of FS 108 that may be closed. If the gate is closed, you must park and hike to the trailhead.

From Roanoke take US 220 North to Clifton Forge. Take I-64 East to Exit #37 and follow the above directions.

Snow on the White Rocks Tower Trail.

<u>Trail Description</u>

The White Rocks Tower Trail is located at the lower trailhead for the Rich Hole Trail. The Tower Trail actually forms the southern boundary for the Rich Hole Wilderness Area. This trail, a continuation of FS 108, leads to the remains of an old fire tower located at the top of the Pleasant Mill Ridge. The trail is approximately 1.5 miles in length and climbs from about 1,400 feet to approximately 3,000 feet. The climb is fairly gradual with a few short, steep sections.

The trail climbs a rocky road with several switchbacks. At about 0.7 miles there is a forest service gate and beyond the gate, the road is grassy. This section of the road/trail has not felt wheels for some time. There are red oaks and tulip poplars of tremendous size. One oak tree has a circumference of 12 feet and another interesting oak has four trunks coming up from its root base.

Just before reaching the top, there is a permanent campsite on the left side of the road. The camp is just outside the wilderness boundary and is not easy to miss. This campsite includes a table and benches. If planning to spending the night, this would be an excellent location - but remember to bring water.

The trail ends at the top of the Pleasant Mill Ridge (See Pleasant Mill Ridge Trail description) where some remains of an old fire tower still lay. The view from the top is excellent in both winter and summer. To the west is the Rough Mountain Wilderness and further still is Warm Springs Mountain. To the east are North Mountain and the Blue Ridge Mountains. While to the north one can look into the heart of the Rich Hole Wilderness and make plans for other possible outings.

Rough
Mountain
Wilderness

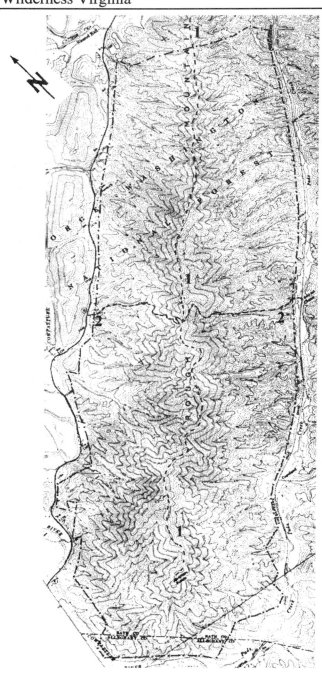

Rough Mountain

Rough Mountain is a large wilderness located approximately seventeen miles east of Covington, Virginia in Alleghany and Bath Counties. This wilderness, in the Warm Springs District of the George Washington National Forest contains 9,300 acres. It was declared a wilderness by Congress in 1987.

This area encompasses most of Rough Mountain including a region called Griffith Knob. Due to the terrain, the wilderness and the mountain seem to be appropriately named. The region is characterized by very steep, dry mountain slopes. The steep terrain creates only limited watershed possibilities and thus there are no major creeks within the wilderness boundaries. To the west the wilderness area is bordered by the Cowpasture River and State Route 42 and to the east it borders Pads Creek and the C&O Railroad.

The wilderness area has only one existing trail. This is the Crane Trail and it runs through the center of the wilderness area, east to west. This trail including a short hike to the trailhead is approximately four miles long. The only other area accessible to hiking due to the steep nature of the terrain and limited access is the ridge top of Rough Mountain. The ridge top is easily accessible from a parking area located just off State Route 42. The hike along the ridge top is about 10.5 miles (one way).

The forest throughout the wilderness is composed of two primary types. The first is the oak-hickory forest so common throughout Virginia. The second is the pine-chestnut oak forest located on dry mountain slopes. The pine suffers severely from the effects of the Southern Pine Bark Beetle, and extensive stands of dead pine are located within the boundaries of the primitive area.

There is one very interesting place in the Rough Mountain Wilderness. Although hard to reach, Griffith Knob has tremendous views to the east, south and west. From the top of Griffith Knob one can also see the Rich Hole Wilderness, Douthat State Park, and the City of Clifton Forge. The Knob also has an abundance of fossils. Finally, this areas rugged beauty is its rough nature. The steep mountainsides create a true sense of wilderness grandeur.

The major drawback to the wilderness is a lack of water. If hiking along the Crane Trail or along the ridge top, take plenty of water. The other major drawback to this wilderness is accessiblity. Most of the land on the west side of the wilderness is posted property and access is restricted. The east side of the wilderness is bordered by the C&O Railroad. Railroad right-of-way is posted and therefore, access is restricted.

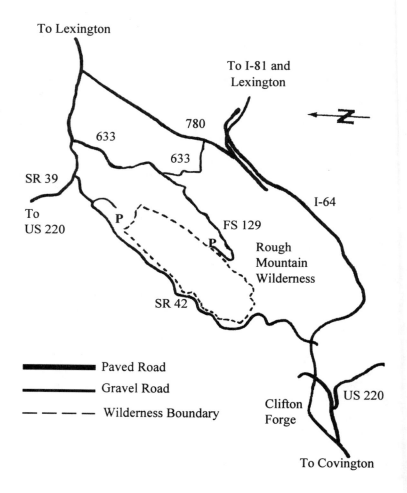

To Lexington

To I-81 and
Lexington

780

633

633

SR 39

I-64

To
US 220

P

FS 129

P

Rough
Mountain
Wilderness

SR 42

Paved Road

Gravel Road

Wilderness Boundary

Clifton
Forge

US 220

To Covington

Crane Trail   1

Length: 4 Miles (One Way)
Time: 2.5 Hours
Elevation Change: 1,170 Feet
Difficulty: Moderately Difficult
USGS Maps: Nimrod Hall, Longdale Furnace
Trailhead: 1.5 Miles From Right Fork on FS129

How To Get There

Take I-81 to I-64 West, Exit #191, at Lexington. Take I-64 to Exit #43 and turn right at the stop sign. Travel 0.3 miles to a stop sign and take a left on CR. 850. Proceed 0.8 miles and turn right onto CR 780. Proceed 1.7 miles and turn left onto CR 633. CR 633 is a dirt road. Travel 4.3 miles to FS129 and take a left. There are two small fords on FS129. Travel 6.3 to a "Y" in the road. Take the right fork which goes uphill. Travel 1.5 miles to a small parking lot near the railroad tracks. This short section of road can be quite muddy when the weather is wet. From the parking area, proceed on foot approximately 1.0 miles in a northerly direction. Follow the tracks to reach the trailhead which is on the opposite side of the tracks from where vehicles are park.

From Roanoke, US 220 to Clifton Forge. Take I-64 East to Exit #43 and turn left. Then follow the above directions.

Trail Description

The Crane Trail cuts across the Rough Mountain Wilderness from the east to the west. The trail's grade is difficult as it climbs from Pads Creek to the top of the Rough Mountain ridge and then descends again to SR 42. The major problem with this trail is there is no access to the trailhead on SR 42. The land along the road is posted by many of the owners. The Crane Trail trailhead is located on land used by a hunting club and the land is posted. Therefore, this trail becomes basically an out and back. The trail starts at an elevation of approximately 1,360 and climbs to a height of 2,530 feet. The elevation near the western end of the trail, near the hunting camp, is about the same elevation as the beginning, 1,360 feet. However, the hike is still pleasant and worth the effort.

The hike begins before reaching the trailhead. At the railroad tracks, a short walk of approximately 1.0 mile, north, is required to reach the trailhead. The trailhead is located just on the other side of the small RR bridge. One note of caution: Railroad property is posted and trespassing can carry a fine. After crossing the bridge, the Forest Service information center is located on the left. The trail heads in a westerly direction from the trailhead. The trail is maintained but can be difficult to see due to leaves and little use.

The path follows a small creek up the side of Rough Mountain. The path is on the right side of the creek. There is a mixture of evergreen and hardwoods at the beginning of the trail. Hemlock, white pine, Virginia pine, maple, and oak are the dominant species. There are some trees down across the trail, but the trail is basically clear of downfall. The trail crosses two smaller tributaries of a larger stream. The ridge across the creek is quite steep, however the angle of the trail is still fairly flat. When the trail veers to the right and heads away from the stream, the climb becomes steep and difficult. There are several switchbacks throughout this part of the path. The first is to the right, followed by one to the left. This area is rocky and dry so the hardwoods thin out and are replaced by Virginia pine and pitch pine. Just before the top, there is a right hand switchback.

At the top, there is a small grassy area with both pine and hardwood. There is a good place to camp at the ridge top, however, water is scarce. The distance from the trailhead to the top is 1.6 miles. A hike in a southerly direction at the top leads to Griffith Knob (See Rough Mountain Trail description).

The trip down the west side of Rough Mountain begins with a switchback to the left followed by a switchback to the right. The trail's grade is fairly easy even though the ridge drops off quickly. The trail passes a small rock river and enters a rhododendron thicket. Once through the thicket, the trail is covered with leaves and the switchbacks are left behind while the footpath follows a shoulder of the mountain.

When the trail bends left, there is a steep descent to the SR 42. This descent becomes more moderate just prior to reaching the wilderness boundary. There are posted signs at the wilderness boundary. If you continue, without permission, trepassers can be charged. The trail ends up in the parking lot for the a hunting club located on SR 42. The distance from the top to SR 42 is 1.4 miles

A rattlesnake sunning itself on some rocks.

Rough Mountain Trail/Bushwhack   2

Length: 10.5 Miles (One Way)
Time: All day and maybe even overnight
Difficulty: Very Difficult
Elevation Change: 1,350 Feet
USGS Map: Nimrod Hall, Longdale Furnace
Trailhead: Off SR 42

How To Get There

Take I-81 to I-64 West, Exit #191 at Lexington. Take Exit #29, at the stop sign, turn north on SR 42. Proceed 15.1 miles to a small dirt road on the right. Turn right and proceed 0.2 miles. Parking can be found on the left. Please remember not to block access through the gate at the end of the road.

From Roanoke, take US 220 to Clifton Forge. Take I-64 East to Exit #29 at the stop sign, turn north on SR 42. Then follow the above directions.

<u>Trail Description</u>

This trail can best be described as a road, and then a bushwhack to the top of the ridge. Once on the ridge top, it becomes a series of game and hunting trails which at times are indistinct and hard to see. The major problem with this hike is the ridge. The ridge is not a gradual climb to a high point, but rather a series of climbs and descents, to the end to the mountain and Griffith Knob. Remember to pack water as the region is dry and there is very little water. Now lets talk about the positive aspects of the climb. First, if you seek solitude, you will find it on this hike. In fact, you probably will not see another soul during the duration of the hike. Second, the scenery is great. One could probably see scenery like this on easier hikes, but the end result is a wonderful reminder of the scenic beauty which Virginia has to offer. This trail is recommended for anyone seeking remote and out of the way places.

The trail begins by crossing a Forest Service gate. There is a small creek on the left and the area is dominated by white pine, tulip poplar, and white oak. As the road moves up higher onto the side of the mountain, the ridge becomes drier and the earlier species are replaced by pine and chestnut oak. At approximately 0.75 miles the road comes to an abrupt end, however, continue walking to the ridge top. This is a short bushwhack (0.25 miles). Once on the ridgetop turn left and head in a southerly direction.

A short distance up the ridge, there is a good view of Cowpasture Valley and Warm Springs Mountain. The ridge top is dominated by oak and hickory on the eastern slope and laurel thickets on the western slope. The laurel thickets have a good undergrowth of huckleberry and blueberry plants. As the slopes become more rocky, the hardwoods are replaced by pines. There is a small grass covered clearing with many small flowering plants, and just beyond this clearing is a sign announcing the boundary for the wilderness area. The sign is located approximately 2.6 miles from the trailhead. Near the sign is a large gnarled hickory whose top has been knocked out and a very large chestnut oak with a split trunk. Warm Springs Mountain can be seen to the west.

Next, is a short steep climb to a beautiful flat area. This flat area becomes quite wide and is the home of many large chestnut oak. After another steep climb, there is a small knoll characterized by many dead and dying pine, victims of the Southern Pine Bark Beetle. There is also a beautiful grassy area with an excellent view to the southwest. This is a great area for camping, but once again there is no water.

After leaving the grassy area, scrub pine dominate the region which makes travel more difficult. The best course of action is to stay with the ridge top. Take heart as the thicket is not large. Once out of the thicket, there is another climb. At the top of this rise there is a good view of the Goshen Pass and the Blue Ridge Mountains to the east. The Rich Hole Wilderness and Pleasant Mill Ridge are visible to the southeast. After a small descent, there is another short steep climb to another wide flat area covered with huge vine thickets. This is a rare sight on a ridge top. There is also a permanent hunting stand in this area. Beyond this area is another small descent followed by another short steep climb. At the ridge top is a small grass clearing. The next climb leads to a hillside covered with laurel and another grassy knoll.

At approximately 5.9 miles the Crane Trail is reached (See Crane Trail description). The Crane Trail is the only maintained trail in the wilderness. There is a spot to camp at the junction with the Crane Trail. Remember, there is no water along the ridge so pack enough water for the duration of the trip. Another small climb leads to a very steep drop to a small saddle. This drop, although long, does not mark the end of the mountain. After the saddle there is a moderate climb.

At the top of the next ridge, there will be two directions from which to choose. Traveling upward and slightly to the west leads to the highest point in the Rough Mountain Wilderness Area with an elevation of 2,800 feet. To reach Griffith Knob travel in a southeasterly direction. There is a slight descent in this direction followed by a gradual climb. When the sides begin to drop off suddenly in all directions, Griffith Knob is just ahead. From the knob, there are great views to the east, south and west. The town of Clifton Forge is visible, as well as the Cowpasture River and the swinging bridge at Griffith. The view from the knob is definitely worth the trip.

One note about this trail, Griffith Knob is the half-way point. This trail is still an out and back.

Saint Marys Wilderness

Saint Marys

The Saint Marys Wilderness is located approximately fifteen miles south of Staunton, Virginia in the southern corner of Augusta County. It is located in the Pedler District of the George Washington National Forest, and contains 10,090 acres. The Saint Marys Wilderness was created by Congress in 1984.

The wilderness has three high peaks within its boundary. These peaks are Cellar Mountain, Bald Mountain, and Big Spy Mountain. The Saint Marys River is the major drainage for the wilderness and is fed by many smaller creeks within the drainage basin. The Saint Marys River maintain a strong flow throughout the year. Cold Springs drain the western portion of the wilderness. Because of all these creeks, water is readily available. Remember for safety reasons treat the water.

The Saint Marys Wilderness has one of the most extensively maintained trail systems in the Virginia wilderness system. There are approximately twenty-seven miles of trails within the wilderness or near its perimeter. These trails provide excellent access to this unique region. This area is unique because although it has been declared a primitive area, the evidence of man's past is very evident. Extensive mining activities have taken place thoughout the Saint Marys region for many years and the remains of those old operations are still visible today.

The forests of the Saint Marys can be divided into four major groups. The first is the oak-hickory forest which dominates most of Virginia. The second forest type is located on the dry slope of the steep mountain located within the wilderness. These slopes have drier tree species such as chestnut oak and Virginia pine. A third forest ecosystem is the wet sheltered coves like Chimney Branch and Bear Branch. In these coves, tulip poplar, hemlock, and white pine thrive. Some of these trees grow very tall. Finally, there is Big Levels which is the home of many stunted table mountain pine and chestnut oak, as well as numerous other smaller species which purchase a difficult existence in this harsh environment.

There are several interesting sites around the Saint Marys Wilderness. First, the area is the home of many waterfalls. Because of the steep nature of the mountain and the many streams located on the side of these mountain, small waterfalls can be seen in many places. The Saint Marys Falls is the most popular. There are also falls along the Mine Bank Trail and up in the Bear Hollow. The rocks of the Saint Marys are spectacular. The Saint Marys is the wilderness area

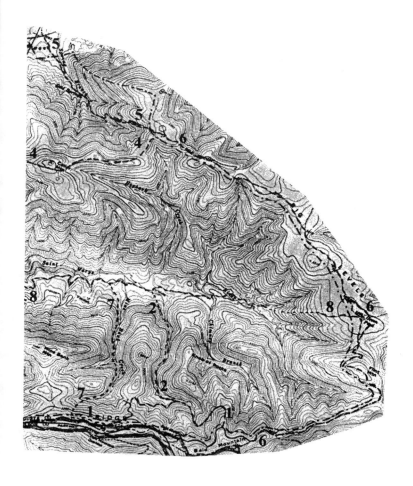

for rock lovers. There are numerous rock slides and rock towers located along many of the trails. Finally, there is Big Levels. Big Levels is a huge flat area located at the top of the northern end of the wilderness. This area sports one of the few natural bodies of water in Virginia. Green Pond, located just outside the wilderness is a small pond in the heart of Big Levels.

The Saint Marys is a popular destination for hikers and campers and is usually very busy, especially around the Saint Marys Falls area. Because of this high use, camping is prohibited around the falls area.

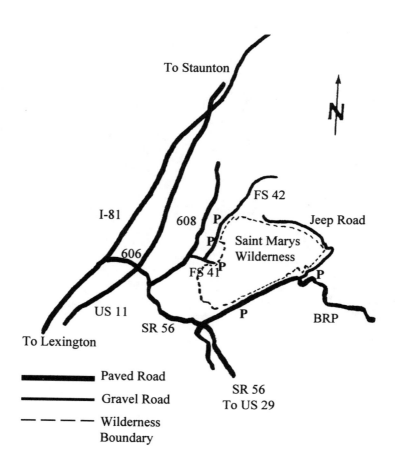

Bald Mountain Trail   1

Length: 1.8 Miles (One Way)
Time: 1 Hour
Elevation Change: 650 Feet
Difficulty: Easy
USGS Map: Vesuvius, Big Levels
Trailhead: Near the Intersection of FS 162 and a Jeep Road

How To Get There

Take the BRP to milepost 22. Near mile post 22, on the north side of the BRP is FS 162. Turn onto FS 162 and proceed about 0.5 miles to the junction of FS 162 and the jeep road. Parking is avavilable where FS 162 and the jeep road intersect. From this parking area, take the right fork and walk about 0.25 miles. Look for the sign indicating the trailhead on the right. Watch for the yellow blazes.

Trail Description

This trail meanders along the side of Bald Mountain before re-joining the Blue Ridge Parkway at the Fork Mountain Overlook near mile post 23. The trailhead is easy to locate on FS 162. The trail is located on the right side of the FS road. Marked with yellow blazes, the trail begins with a gentle drop followed by a gradual climb. A small wilderness sign marks the boundary almost immediately upon beginning the hike.

The trail begins with a long descent through a laurel thicket. The path makes a right switchback near two very large trees. Beyond the trees the trail continues its descent to a small stream. Near the stream are many large rocks and some large hemlock. The trail crosses the stream and meanders along the left bank. There are some trees down across the trail in this location.

The path crosses two small creeks. Shortly, after crossing the second creek, there is an old road which parallels the Bear Branch (See Bear Hollow Bushwhack description). The Bald Mountain trail continues left along the mountainside, becoming flatter and entering a small clearing. Shortly (25 yards), the trail begins to climb up the ridge and the grade increases slightly. After crossing a creek there is a yellow blaze. The trail turns right, and there is a three-log-bridge over another small stream. When the path crosses over yet another stream, small hemlock trees line the sides of the trail. The grade increases a little but the walk is still easy. The trail narrows and passes through a tunnel of mountain laurel and rhododendron.

About 0.5 miles from the junction with the Bear Hollow Bushwhack the path opens up again. Oak and hickory dominate the forest. Another yellow blaze is visible when the trail crests a small rise and turns to the left. Here the path could be described as an old road. There is a great deal of down fall littering the forest. The trail turns back to the right, and there are many blazes along the way. A nice campsite is loacted beyond an earthen barrier left behind by bulldozers.

Two more earthen barriers are crossed just past the campsite. After passing a National Park Service sign, signifying the Blue Ridge Parkway is near, the trail turns right. The trail reaches the Parkway appoximately 1.25 miles from the junction with the Bear Hollow Bushwhack

Bear Hollow Bushwhack   2

Length: 2 Miles (One Way)
Time: 1.5 hours
Elevation Change: 560 Feet
Difficulty: Downhill But Difficult
USGS Map: Vesuvius, Big Levels
Trailhead: Via the Bald Mountain Trail

How To Get There

Via the Bald Mountain Trail.

Trail Description

The trail is fairly easy to follow as there is an old road to follow almost all the way to an old mining camp along the Saint Marys Trail. This is a great place for the intrepid hiker; someone who is willing to put up with a little difficulty. Bear Branch cascades down the side of Bald Mountain eventually reaching the Saint Marys River. The sheltered hollow of the creek is the home of large hemlock, white pine, and many types of hardwoods. There are a few nice waterfalls on the Bear Branch as well as some beautiful and remote campsites.

The trail begins as a gradual descent but becomes steep as the creek begins to drop to the Saint Marys River. First, the trail crosses three small creeks. A small hunting camp is located near the second creek. Throughout the area there are large maple, birch, hemlock, and white pine. After crossing the third creek, the road becomes less visible and harder to follow. There is also a large amount of brush lying across the road.

At approximately 1.0 miles, the road disappears altogether. At this point, it is best to stay on the left side of the creek. After about 0.1 miles, the road reappears. There is a nice series of waterfalls along this portion of the bushwhack. Finally, the hollow opens out into a nice wide area. The road again disappears among the laurel thickets along the creek. To get to the Saint Marys Trail, parallel the creek. The Bear Branch crosses the Saint Marys Trail near the site of an old mining operation.

Blacksnakes can be found throughout the wilderness areas.

Big Spy Mountain Trail   3

Length: 1.5 Miles One Way
Time: 2 Hours
Elevation Change: 300 Feet
Difficulty: Easy
USGS Map: Vesuvius, Big Levels
Trailhead: Near 25 Mile Post on the BRP

How To Get There

Take the BRP to a small parking area on the west side of the Parkway between mile posts 25 and 26. There are two FS gates at the parking area. Remember not to block the gates.

Trail Description

The Big Spy Mountain Trail, although not located on any maps is very pleasant. The trail, a short 1.5 miles, travels out to the end of a rock outcrop which offers a spectacular view. There is a steep drop to a saddle but the elevation change is not very great. Along the trail, is a forest comprised of trees which like a drier climate. Some of the trees include Virginia pine and chestnut oak. This region is very dry so pack water.

The beginning of the trail may be on posted property, and there are signs which indicate the property is private. To avoid the private property, travel downhill to signs of a recent survey and bear to the left following the contour. This leads to an old road grade. This bypass is a bushwhack. If you choose to go on the road, bypass the first right. At the "Y" in the road, bear to the right. The trail begins with a gradual descent. There is some brush and fallen trees across the trail, but travel is not difficult. Beyond the brush the trail drops quickly. There is a switchback to the left, then one to the right and then another to the left.

Upon reaching the saddle, the trail flattens out. The forest consists of chestnut oak and pine with mountain laurel dominating the understory. When the saddle has been traversed, the climb up Big Spy Mountain begins. The trail is at times difficult to see, so be alert for changes in the trail's direction. After the first steep climb, the trail bears to the left, and then a short downhill section past a boulder pile on the right. This is followed by an easy uphill section. Next, there is a short steep section up a rock river. Four large boulders on the right are the gateway to the top. Just beyond the these rocks is the end of Big Spy Mountain. The end of Big Spy Mountain is a large rock outcrop which provides an excellent view to the south and west. There is a wide, steep boulder field on the west side of the mountain. There is an excellent view of Little Spy Mountain and Cellar Mountain from this location.

Cellar Mountain Trail   4

Length: 3.2 Miles
Time: 2 Hours
Elevation Change: 1,250 Feet
Difficulty: Difficult
USGS Map: Vesuvius, Big Levels
Trailhead: FS 42

How To Get There

Take I-81 to Exit #205, south of Staunton. If traveling south on I-81 turn left on CR 606 or if traveling North on I-81 turn right. Proceed 1.5 miles east to Steeles Tavern. At the "T" intersection on US 11, turn left. Travel approximately 100 yards and turn right on SR 56. Travel 1.2 miles, cross the South River and turn left on CR 608. Proceed 2.2 miles to a yield sign. Turn right under a train tressel and continue on CR 608. Travel 2.6 miles to FS 41 and turn right. Proceed 0.6 miles to FS 42 and turn left. The parking area is located on the right 0.8 miles from the intersection of FS 42 and FS 41.

Trail Description

The Cellar Mountain Trail climbs rapidly from FS 42 to the top of Cellar Mountain and then lazily meanders across the top of the mountain to the junction of a jeep road and the Cold Springs Trail. The trail is marked with blue blazes. This first part of the trail is extremely steep and very difficult. There are many switchbacks during the first 2.2 miles. The trail passes near the top of Cellar Mountain which is the highest point in the Saint Marys Wilderness with an elevation of 3,645 feet.

The trail begins at a parking area on FS 42 which includes a Forest Service information center and a livestock fence. The beginning of the trail is usually wet in the winter and early summer. Shortly after crossing the trail guard, there is a sign marking Saint Marys Wilderness boundary. The trail begins with moderate grade passing through a forest of mixed hardwoods and pines. There is a small spring on the left just before the big climb. Take advantage of this spring because it is the last water spot on the trail. The spring is 0.5 miles from the trailhead.

Beyond the spring the grade of the trail becomes steep. There is a switchback to the left and then a long, steep, rocky, straight stretch through small pitch pine and mountain laurel. The grade is now very steep. After a switchback to the right there is a nice view to the south. The next switchback to the left has a rock outcrop and a good view. Low pines continue to dominate this dry area. After a right switchback there is an area covered with ferns and running cedar. There are many large colonies of ants throughout the climb. There is switchback to the right, then to the left, and then again to the right. In this area is a nice view of the Blue Ridge to the south and the mountains of the Alleghenys to the west. There is one more switchback to the right and then one more to the left. In all there is a total of 9 switchbacks.

At 2.2 miles the trail begins to level out. There are some small rock spurs on the right and a spot for camping close to the rocks. There is a great panoramic view into the Saint Marys from the rocks. The trail begins a series of ups and downs near the crest of Cellar Mountain, 2.3 miles. There are many low shrubs of mountain laurel and rhododendron. Teaberry can be found growing on the ground, and tree species include oak, maple, hickory, and a few unusual species like table mountain pine and chinkapin.

The trail begins a easy descent to a saddle, at 2.8 miles. Beyond the saddle, the trail begins to climb again. There is as nice panorama into the Saint Marys. Then there is another easy climb to the jeep road. Just before the jeep road, is a wilderness boundary sign and a trail sign. At the road (See Jeep Trail description), a right, leads to the Parkway 5.9 miles away. A left at the road leads to the Cold Springs Trail about 100 yards away (See Cold Springs Trail description).

Cold Springs Trail   5

Length: 1.4 miles
Time: 1 Hour
Elevation Change: 1,300 Feet
Difficulty: Moderate/Diffcult
USGS Maps: Big Level, Vesuvius
Trailhead: FS 42

How To Get There

Take I-81 to Exit #205, south of Staunton. If traveling south on I-81 turn left on CR 606. If traveling North on I-81 turn right. Proceed 1.5 miles east to Steeles Tavern. At the "T" intersection on US 11, turn left. Travel approximately 100 yards and turn right on SR 56. Travel 1.2 miles, cross the South River and turn left on CR 608. Proceed 2.2 miles to a yield sign. Turn right under a train tressel and continue on CR 608. Travel 2.6 miles to FS 41 and turn right. Proceed 0.6 miles and turn left on FS 42. Travel 2.6 miles to a small parking area on the right.

Poison ivy near a trail in the Saint Marys.

Trail Description

The Cold Springs Trail is a beautiful pathway that travels from FS 42, to the ridge top and intersection with the Cellar Mountain Trail and the jeep road. The trail is steep, at times, but the beautiful views provide plenty of incentive to keep climbing. The scenery includes a small pond and large rock outcropping. As the trail makes its way up one side of a deep canyon there is a distinctive western mountain feel. Access to the trail is hindered by the fact that the trailhead is located on private property. To avoid crossing this property, park 0.5 miles from the trailhead and follow the National Forest property boundary southeast and then northeast until it intersects with the trail. The junction will be obvious as the trail is very wide near the beginning.

The first part of the trail, up to the small pond, travels up a creek runoff area and, at times, can be quite wet. There is a large amount of undergrowth, so traveling off-trail to avoid the water is limited. This section of the trail is wide and easy to follow. At about 0.65 miles, there is an old rock wall which is actually a dam for the pond. This is not Green Pond which is announced on the sign at the beginning of the hike. The pool is pleasant and a nice spot to have a snack and filter some drinking water for the climb ahead.

From the pond the trail grade becomes more difficult. At a little over 1.0 miles the path leads past some fallen rock. Just beyond this rock pile, 1.2 miles, is a left handed switchback. The trail crosses a rock river - remember to be careful - the trail looks like it might go straight across these rocks. A spur does cross this area and goes down to the stream, but the Cold Springs Trail follows a switchback and climbs up and away from the stream. There is a wall of rocks to the right and the trail will make a wide right "U" turn around the small rock outcrop. The side of the ridge becomes steep and drops off quickly to the right. The view is great. At about 1.4 miles there is a large outcropping in the canyon. The vegetation becomes thick and the trail narrows substantially. At this point the grade becomes steep and remains this way until the junction with Jeep Trail and Cellar Mountain Trail. Remember to drink plenty of water during the climb. The trail makes another left switchback followed by a long, wide right turn. The trail continues its steep ascent. At about 2.0 miles there are hemlock on the right, and shortly after these trees there is a sign with an arrow pointing back down the trail. Rejoice in the observance of this sign - the climb is almost over.

At 2.1 miles the trail intersects with the Cellar Mountain Trail and the jeep road. To the right there is a barricade and wilderness sign. This is the Cellar Mountain Trail (See Cellar Mountain Trail desceription) which travels 3.2 miles down to FS 42, about 1.8 miles from the Cold Springs trailhead. This makes a very nice loop. The fire road is muddy and generally unpleasant. However, it does lead to Green Pond and the Saint Marys Trail as well as other trails (See Jeep Trail description). If planning to descend via the Cold Springs take it slow; the steep descent can be very tough on hips, knees, and ankles.

Jeep Trail   6

Length: 5.9 Miles
Time: 3 Hours
Elevation Change: 370 Feet
Difficulty: Easy
USGS Map: Vesuvius, Big Levels
Trailhead: Near the Intersection of FS 162 and a Jeep Road

How To Get There

Take the BRP to mile post 22. Near mile post 22, on the north side of the Parkway is FS 162. Turn onto FS 162 and proceed about 0.5 miles to the junction of FS 162 and the jeep road. Parking is avavilable where FS 162 and the jeep road intersect.

Trail Description

This trail is actually a road across Big Levels, a high flat area on the northern end of the wilderness area. Although the jeep trail is not located in the wilderness, it serves to connect many trails. The jeep trail ties together the Bald Mountain Trail, the Saint Marys Trail, the Cellar Mountain Trail and the Cold Springs Trail. It begins near mile post 22 on the BRP. From the Parkway it heads in a westerly direction to the junction with Cold Springs Trail and the Cellar Mountain Trail. Heading west, the grade is marked by a gradual descent.

The first section of the trail is the steepest, and the road has some switchbacks. The switches start about 1.5 miles from the BRP. Once through the switchbacks, the road levels out and passes north of Green Pond and the Saint Marys Trailhead, approximately 2.9 miles. Finally, the jeep trail reaches the trails on the western end of the wilderness. There is a turn around area at the end of the road, and it is heavily littered. The trailhead for the Cellar Mountain Trail and the Cold Springs Trail are located at the end of the Jeep Trail.

Cellar Mountain

Mine Bank Trail   7

Length: 3.0 Miles (One Way)
Time: 1.5 Hours
Elevation Change: 1,025 Feet
Difficulty: Moderate/Difficult
USGS Map: Big Levels
Trailhead: Near Milepost 23 on the Blue Ridge Parkway

How To Get There

Near milepost 23 at the Fork Mountain Overlook.

Trail Description

The Mine Bank is a beautiful trail that travels from the BRP down the ridge to the Saint Marys Trail. The trail is marked with orange blazes. Most of the Mine Bank parallels a noisy stream with numerous stair-step waterfalls. The trail is short and makes a great day or afternoon hike. On your way down the ridge make sure to

216

note how steep the trail is as this could be the route back.

From the parking area look for a sign that marks the Mine Bank Trail. After about thirty yards there is another sign that reads Bald Mountain Trails and points right (See Bald Knob Trail description). The Mine Bank goes to the left. The trail begins with an easy grade and the down side of the ridge on the right. At about 0.3 miles there is an orange blaze, and shortly after the blaze there is a wide, right-handed switchback. After a left turn, the grade becomes much steeper, and the trail becomes annoyingly rocky. There is evidence of heavy runoff. Care must be taken in this section to keep from twisting an ankle. At about 0.5 miles the steep section ends. The trail makes a right turn and then it reaches a narrow valley; here in this little valley is the beginning of the Mine Bank Creek. The stream is on the right. As the trail approaches the stream, it enters an area of thin undergrowth and hemlock. The understory quickly closes back in, though, and is comprised many of rhododendron and mountain laurel. After passing a blaze, the trail opens up, again. In this area the trail can be difficult to see so stay to the left and watch for the next blaze. The steep walls of the canyon make the valley shady and cool in the summer. A rock river flows down the mountain on the left. Just beyond this rock river, the trail crosses the creek near a set of short waterfalls. The stream is now on the left. At about 1.3 miles the stream is again crossed. This crossing is especially interesting as it occurs at the top of a fifteen foot section of small falls.

The trail's grade is now moderate and the trail is still descending. Another crossing puts the trail on the right side of the creek. Two different ecosystems thrive in this area: Hardwoods dominate the ridge to the right and hemlock occupy the left ridge. The trail crosses two small feeder creeks and then wanders through a beautiful area where there are rock outcrops on both sides of the stream. These rock outcrops are a familiar sight in the Saint Marys Wilderness and are an integral part of what makes this area unique. The rocks are at about 1.8 miles into the hike.

The grade moderates considerably in this area, even though the stream continues to drop. When the trail wraps around a boulder, the stream falls away sharply to the right. At about 2.1 miles there is another set of falls down to the right. They are hard to see but can be easily heard. To view the falls, walk a short distance beyond the falls, and then walk carefully toward the creek. The angle of the trail remains easy with short steep sections.

At about 2.6 miles hardwoods with a mountain laurel understory begin to dominate the forest. The trail bends left and heads away from the stream. It climbs to a small finger ridge and then begins to drop again. Some sections of the trail in this region can be very wet and muddy. The trail continues to descend and then intersects with the Saint Marys Trail at about 3.0 miles. A left at this intersection leads one to the southern end of the wilderness area and a parking lot on FS 41. A right leads to the northern end of the wilderness area and Green Pond (See Saint Marys Trail description).

The Mine Bank Creek in the Saint Marys.

Saint Marys Trail   8

Length: 6.9 Miles (One Way)
Time: 3.5 Hours
Elevation Change: 1,500 Feet
Difficulty: Moderate
USGS Map: Vesuvius, Big Levels
Trailhead: Parking Area on FS41

How To Get There

Take I-81 to Exit #205, south of Staunton. If traveling south on I-81 turn left on CR 606 or if traveling North on I-81 turn right. Proceed 1.5 miles east to Steeles Tavern. At the "T" intersection wiath US 11, turn left. Travel approximately 100 yards and turn right on SR 56. Travel 1.2 miles, cross the South River and turn left on CR 608. Proceed 2.2 miles to a yield sign. Turn right under a train tressel and continue on CR 608. Travel 2.6 miles to FS 41 and turn right. Proceed travel 1.4 miles to the Saint Marys Trail parking area.

Trail Description

The Saint Marys Trail is a wonderful trail which slowly climbs up to Green Pond, a small natural pond located in Big Levels. The trail, marked with blue blazes, is generally an easy trail to hike with the exception of the creek crossings and the steep climb near the end. The journey from the trailhead to the Levels area is a wonderful experience with many unique natural and man-made formations. The Saint Marys Trail travels through the remains of several old mining areas and the scars of man's activity are still evident. Nature, in its own slow way, is beginning to reclaim the land and hide the traces of this activity.

The trail begins at an elevation of approximately 1,700 feet and climbs to an elevation of 3,200 feet at Green Pond. Most of the climb is done in the last 1.5 miles as the trail crosses the last small stream of the Saint Marys watershed and climbs to the ridge top. The climb is short and very steep. The trail makes extensive use of an old railroad grade along the river.

From the parking lot, the trail begins with a Forest Service information center. After crossing a livestock fence, there is a small sign making the wilderness boundary. The clear, rushing Saint Marys

219

River is on the right. The trail passes over a section that is severely eroded and then enters the forest. The forest is comprised tulip poplar, hemlock, and oak. A small spring crosses the trail and there is evidence of some beaver activity along the river bank. In this area there are signs of old mining activity. The valley is a narrow, steep walled gorge with many rock rivers and small cliffs, and numerous campsites dot the trail edge.

If the water is up at the first of creek crossing, the only way to cross is with bare feet. Once on the other side, the creek is on the left. The trail narrows and erosion is actively cutting the right creek bank, making footing treacherous. Beyond here, at an elevation of 1,900 feet and 1.9 miles from the trailhead is a small clearing with many signs of man's activity. This is the junction with the Saint Marys Falls Trail (See Saint Marys Falls Trail description). The Saint Marys Falls Trail continues to follow the river, while the Saint Marys Trail bears right and follows a small creek. There is a sign with arrows to the BRP and Green Pond.

The trail narrows and becomes steeper as it moves up the hollow. There are some large poplar and hemlock in this area. There is also a campsite near a large rock on the right. A little farther up the trail is a small falls. The falls are about five feet high with a pool of clear water below it.

At a small clearing, about 0.4 miles from the trail junction, the creek is crossed. After crossing the stream, the trail turns left. Beyond the crossing, the trail can be wet and muddy. Upon entering a steep walled canyon, the trail climbs rapidly. Although, the climb is steep it is also short. After a switchback to the left, the grade moderates.

At the top of this climb there is an old mining site with an old settling pond. The trail is a little confusing in this region, so be careful. Follow the trail to the back of the pond site. Once on the other side of the pond, the trail begins to descend. A small creek is crossed and then it parallels the trail on the left. On the other side of the creek, the trail begins to climb, but the grade is moderate. Throughout the area there are small hemlock, oak, and popular. The ground cover is blueberry and teaberry. The teaberry is a delicious snack in the early days of the spring.

The trail descends again to another creek. At the crossing, the trail bends to the right. The Saint Marys River is audible to the left. Another small creek is crossed and an old road exits to the right. This road leads to the site of more mining activity. The road is 3.9 miles from the trailhead. There is a campsite and a small spring in this area. Just beyond this road is the junction with the Mine Bank Trail (See Mine Bank Trail description). This trail is located 2.3 miles from the junction with the Saint Marys Falls Trail at an elevation of 2,200 feet. The Mine Bank Trail exits the Saint Marys Trail to the right.

Beyond the Mine Bank Trail, the Saint Marys Trail is fairly level. At 4.7 miles the Bear Branch is crossed two times, but the crossings are not difficult. The are some nice falls up the Bear Branch for those willing to do some bushwacking (See Bear Hollow Bushwhack description). After crossing the Bear Branch the second time, another old mining operation is visible. There are many gullies and mounds of dirt as well as some old concrete pillars and footings. There are several nice campsites located in a this old mining camp. The trail climbs a little when leaving the mining site but quickly levels out again, and the sounds of the river return.

Once beyond this mining area, the Saint Marys River quickly loses its strength. There are several small creeks to cross including the Saint Marys, and large thickets of rhododendron dominate the landscape. Just prior to the last creek crossing, the trail begins to climb rapidly. The Saint Marys River is now quite small. This last creek crossing is 5.4 miles from the trailhead. The trail grade is difficult as it begins to climb to Big Levels and Green Pond. A big rock in the middle of the trail is located at approximately the halfway point of the climb. There are many small pine and chestnut oak.

Upon reaching the ridge top, after a climb of 0.9 miles, the trail flattens out and is very level. There are many small trees and low bushes. Approximately 0.5 miles after reaching the top, there is a Saint Marys Wilderness sign and a Forest Service information center. Green Pond is located just beyond the sign, and there are several places to camp. The Green Pond is located 2.4 miles from the junction of the Mine Branch Trail at an elevation of 3,200 feet. The trail passes Green Pond to the left and at 0.3 miles is the junction with the Jeep Trail. A right leads to the BRP and a left leads to the Cellar Mountain Trail and the Cold Springs Trail (See Jeep Trail description).

The St. Marys Falls

Saint Marys Falls Trail   9

Length: 0.5 Miles
Time: 30 Minutes
Elevation Change: 150 Feet
Difficulty: Easy
USGS Map: Vesuvius, Big Levels
Trailhead: Parking Area on FS41

How to Get There

Via the St. Marys Trail.

Trail Description

The Falls Trail begins at the intersection of the Saint Marys Trail and the Saint Marys Falls Trail. This junction is reached by walking 1.9 miles up the Saint Marys Trail. This trail is a short 0.5 miles and travels along the Saint Marys River. The trail grade is very easy as it wanders through a narrow, steep walled gorge lined with many towering cliffs and imposing rock rivers. The path terminates at the Saint Marys Falls, a small waterfall about 15 feet high.

At the junction of the Saint Marys Trail and the Saint Marys Falls Trail, hike toward the Saint Marys River. After 100 yards the river has to be forded. It is possible to cross the river without taking boots off when the stream is low, but when the creek is up expect to get wet. Once on the other side, there is a nice campsite on the right. Thoughout this area there are many cliffs and rock towers. The trail is lined with laurel thickets, small oak, and chestnut. The path goes through a very narrow gorge and some large cliffs can be seen on the right. In the area of the gorge there is a stream entering from the right on the opposite side of the river. Here, the remains of some old concrete pillars are visible. They were utilized when the region was extensively mined.

The creek must be forded again just before the falls. This ford may be possible without removing footwear, especially a little farther up the creek. The trail traverses a small bend to the right just prior to the falls. At the falls, there is a tall hemlock and a tall rock tower. For those who like to climb, this cliff is suitable for some top roping. Although there are several choice spots for camping, camping is not permited in this area.

There are other campsites above the falls on the other side of the river. The trail continues on up the river for some distance. This is a continuation of the old railroad grade which the Saint Marys Trail follows.

The Saint Marys Trail combined with the Falls Trail make an excellent day hike for most any hiking group. The trail is not too long nor too strenuous. The only major difficulty is the fording.

Shawvers Run Wilderness

Shawvers Run

Shawvers Run is a small wilderness located approximately thirty miles northwest of Roanoke. This wilderness is located in the New Castle District of the Thomas Jefferson National Forest and encompasses an area of about 3,570 acres. The area was designated a wilderness by Congress in 1987.

The Shawvers Run Wilderness is located on the western side of Potts Mountain and includes a long spur on the west side of the mountain. This spur creates the drainage basins for the two major creeks in the region. Shawvers Run drains the northeastern area of the wilderness; while Valley Branch drains the southwestern portion of Shawvers Run Wilderness. Even though both of these creeks are small, water does flow year round.

The wilderness is completely undeveloped and has no existing maintained trail system, but there are several old roads located throughout the wilderness. These roads provide fairly easy access into the heart of the Shawvers Run. The roads, along with some short cross country hikes, provide plenty of hiking for the avid back woods hiker. In fact, there are over ten miles of unmarked trails, which follow the old road grades. The area is seldom visited, except during hunting season, and thus it provides plenty of quiet, undisturbed hiking.

The forest is composed of three different ecosystems. The first is composed of trees found in the sheltered cove of Valley Branch. Here the cove hardwoods such as poplar and birch, as well as evergreens like hemlock and white pine, thrive. The second forest type is the oak-hickory forests which dominates most of the mountains in Virginia today. The third major ecosystem is located on the dry exposed spur to the west of Potts Mountain. In this area, Virginia pine and chestnut oak dominate the overstory. Also scattered throughout the area are understory species like dogwood, striped maple, rhododendron, mountain laurel, and serviceberry.

There are several interesting locations within the Shawvers Run Wilderness. The first is a narrow walled canyon which Valley Branch flows through. This sheltered canyon is covered with lush and green foliage. The one major difficulty with the area is its remoteness. The second area is Hanging Rock. This rock outcrop overlooks the Hanging Rock Valley. On clear days it is possible to see the Blue Ridge Mountains in the east and West Virginia to the west. A third interesting area is the saddle region. There is a clearing at the end of the high spot in the middle of the wilderness and just below the ridge

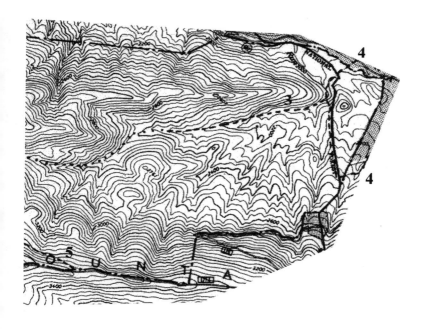

top is an impact carter from a fighter jet crash in 1993.

Two notes of caution about this wilderness area. Please be careful during hunting season. There are two hunting camps located on the southern boundary of the wilderness area. The first is near the end of the trail which leads down to the Valley Branch. The second is located where the Valley Branch exits the small canyon. Also, be careful of rattlesnakes. There are rattlesnakes within the wilderness area. This should not come as a surprise since rattlesnakes can be found in many parts of Virginia. We only mention this as several were seen one afternoon while hiking.

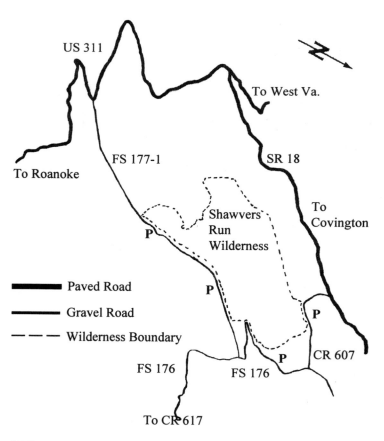

Hanging Rock Trail   1

Length: 0.4 of a Mile (One Way)
Time: 1 Hour
Elevation Change: 150 Feet
Difficulty: Easy
USGS Map: Potts Creek
Trailhead: FS 177-1

How To Get There

Take I-64 West to Covington. Take Exit #16 and turn right at the stop sign. At the stop light, turn left. Travel 1.0 mile and turn left at the stop light. This is SR 18. Travel 20.6 miles and turn left on CR 607. Travel 1.4 miles and turn right on CR 681. Travel 3.3 miles to the top of Potts Mountain. Turn right on FS 177-1. Travel 3.4 miles to a parking area on the right.

From Roanoke, take I-81 to Exit #140and travel north on US 311. Take US 311 to the top of Potts Mountain and turn right on FS 177-1. FS 177-1 actually continues straight and US 311 bends to the left. Proceed 3.6 miles to a small parking area on the left.

Trail Description

This trail is a very short out and back which ends at Hanging Rock, a rock outcrop overlooking the Hanging Rock Valley. The trailhead is located on the right side of FS 177-1.

The trail begins with a very easy climb through mixed hardwoods and rhododendron. It winds in a southwesterly direction toward Hanging Rock. Although not marked, the trail's direction is clear. When the path begins to descend , small rock outcroppings are visible on the left. Just beyond these small rock cliffs is Hanging Rock. The view from Hanging Rock is spectacular. To the northwest, is the Shawvers Run Wilderness. The long ridge to the southeast is Potts Mountain, while the ridge to the west is Peters Mountain. The valley in the middle of these two mountains is the Hanging Rock Valley.

Saddle Trail 2

Length: 1.0 Miles (One Way)
Time: 1 Hour
Elevation Change: 100 Feet
Difficulty: Easy
USGS Map: Potts Creek
Trailhead: FS 177-1

How To Get There

Take I-64 West to Covington. Take Exit #16 and turn right at the stop sign. At the stop light, turn left. Travel 1.0 mile and turn left at the stop light. This is SR 18. Travel 20.6 miles and turn left on CR 607. Travel 1.4 miles and turn right on SR 681. Travel 3.3 miles to the top of Potts Mountain. Turn right on FS 177-1. Proceed 1.6 miles to a small parking area on the right.

From Roanoke, take I-81 to Exit #140 and travel north on US 311. Take US 311 to the top of Potts Mountain and turn right on FS 177-1. FS 177-1 actually continues straight and US 311 bends to the left. Proceed 5.4 miles to a small parking area on the left.

Trail Description

The Saddle Trail is a short trail across a saddle to an area with an elevation of approximately 3,400 feet in the heart of the Shawvers Run Wilderness. The Saddle Trail is reached via the Valley Branch Trail located on FS 177-1. This trail is easy with only a slight gains and losses in elevation. The path is narrow and at times hard to follow, as it winds its way to a shoulder on the west side of Potts Mountain.

Th trailhead is reached by hiking approximately 0.25 miles down the Valley Branch Trail. The trailhead is difficult to see, but will be on the right just after passing a large rock on the left. Once the trailhead is located, the trail descends at a moderate grade through a forest of small mixed hardwoods. The trail quickly flatten out and traverses a small saddle. This saddle is approximately 0.2 miles from the trailhead. To the left is the watershed for Valley Branch and to the right is the watershed for Shawvers Run.

There is short climb followed by an easy descent. There is another short climb to a rocky spot shaded by chestnut oak. This last climb is gradual and heads to a small overgrown clearing at the summit of the shoulder. To the right and slightly downhill from this clearing is an impact crater created by jet crash in the fall of 1993.

A flame Azalea

Shawvers Run Trail/ Bushwhack   3

Length: 2.8 Miles (One Way)
Time: 5 Hours
Elevation Change: 1,275 Feet
Difficulty: Difficult
USGS Map: Potts Mountain
Trailhead: Route 607

How To Get There

Take I-64 West to Covington. Take Exit #16 and turn right at the stop sign. At the stop light, turn left. Travel 1.0 mile and turn left at the stop light. This is SR 18. Travel 20.6 miles and turn left on CR 607. Proceed 1.0 mile to a parking area on the right. There is a parking area on the right a lower parking area for the FS 176 Trail is located 1.0 miles on the right from this intersection.

From Roanoke, take I-81 to exit #140 and travel north on US 311 to SR 18. Turn right on SR 18 and proceed 6.3 miles to CR 607. Then follow the above directions.

Trail Description

This trail begins at a small parking area on the right side of CR 607. From the parking area, the trail immediately enters the woods. The trail, which is actually an old road grade, follows a small branch; the grade is gentle and the hiking is easy. The trail crosses a small feeder creek and then forks. A left at the fork leads to a parking area on FS 176(See Trail on FS 176 description). Take the right fork which leads to Shawvers Run.

Shortly after the fork, the trail crosses Shawvers Run. The path winds through a dense rhododendron thicket with cove hardwoods towering overhead. The creek is on the left. This old road has a moderate grade and ends after about 1.0 mile. When the road plays out, cross the creek. There is an old wagon road which leads to an area just below the saddle. This wagon road is very indistinct and hard to follow. However, it does wind its way through an area which is overgrown with small mountain laurel. Eventually, the wagon road disappears altogether. At this point, it becomes a bushwhack to the saddle. The laurel is not overwhelming but does make for difficult hiking.

Near the saddle, the ridge becomes steep. However, this area is home to many very large hardwoods and the thickets of laurel gradually disappear. Once at the saddle, there are several options to continue the hike. (See Saddle Trail and the Valley Branch Area to get some ideas.)

Trail on FS 176   4

Length: 1.7 Miles (One Way)
Time: 1 Hours
Elevation Change: 325 Feet
Difficulty: Easy
USGS Map: Potts Creek
Trailhead: County Route 607 and FS 176

How To Get There

Take I-64 West to Covington. Take Exit #16 and turn right at the stop sign. At the stop light, turn left. Travel 1.0 mile and turn left at the stop light. This is SR 18. Travel 20.6 miles and turn left on CR 607. The lower parking area for the FS 176 Trail is located 1.0 miles on the right from this intersection. From the intersection with

CR 607, proceed 1.4 miles and turn right on CR 681. Travel 0.4 miles to a parking area on the right. This parking area is the area where the trail description begins.

From Roanoke, take I-81 to Exit #140 and take US 311 North. Travel 1.3 miles and take a left at the stop light. Proceed 24 miles and turn right on CR 611. Travel 5 miles and turn left on CR 617. Travel 2.3 miles to FS 176 and turn left. After cresting the mountain, continue down the other side 2.9 miles to a parking area on the left.

<u>Trail Description</u>

This trail leads from the parking area on FS 176 to the parking area on CR 607. The trail wanders through an oak-hickory forest descending from the trailhead to one of the small feeder creeks of Shawvers Run. The trail passes through two very distinct areas: the first is a dry upper slope and the second is a moist creek basin.

The trail begins by crossing a Forest Service gate on FS176. Initially, it is an old road which travels through an area of small mixed hardwoods and scrub pine. There is an easy climb at the beginning of the trail, and the climb continues until reaching an open area.

After passing through the open area, the trail forks. The trail which continues straight ahead is the trail to follow. The trail which forks to the right loops back to the main trail. The old road disappears and the trail becomes a small footpath. After crossing a small creek it forks again. The straight fork is a dead end. The right fork proceeds through an area of pine, laurel, and chestnut oak.

The trail starts to descend after leaving the second fork behind. There is a switchback to the right and the trail enters a park like area of large cove hardwoods. This area is approximately 0.8 miles from the trailhead. The are several campsites in this area and water is readily available. However, remember to treat all water before consuming it. Just beyond this area, the trail again becomes an old road bed. There are many small hardwoods which slowly give way to pines thickets.

The trail crosses a small creek. Just beyond the creek an old road exits to the right. This road ends quickly but it can be utilized for a bushwhack back to FS 176. Just beyond this road is a trail to the right. This trail leads to Shawvers Run and continues about a mile up the Run (See Shawvers Run Trail description). The trail crosses another small branch before joining CR 607.

The Valley Branch area seen from Hanging Rock.

Valley Branch Access Trail   5

Length: 2.7 Miles
Time: 1.5 Hours
Elevation Change: 1,300 Feet
Difficulty:Moderate
USGS Map: Potts Creek
Trailhead: FS177-1

How To Get There

Take I-64 West, to Covington. Take Exit #16 and turn right at the stop sign. At the stop light, turn left. Travel 1.0 mile and turn left at the stop light. This is SR 18. Travel 20.6 miles and turn left on CR 607. Travel 1.4 miles and turn right on SR 681. Travel 3.3 miles to the top of Potts Mountain. Turn right on FS 177-1. Proceed 1.6 miles to a small parking area on the right.

From Roanoke, take I-81 to Exit #140 and travel north on US 311. Take US 311 to the top of Potts Mountain and turn right on FS 177-1. FS 177-1 actually continues straight and US 311 bends to the left. Proceed 5.4 miles to a small parking area on the left.

Trail Description

This trail is an old road which travels from the top of Potts Mountain to the Valley Branch near the southern end of the Shawvers Run Wilderness Area. The road is in good condition and the hiking is easy. The trail gradually descends down the side of Potts Mountain and is an out and back, unless it is combined with a hike up an old wagon road along the Valley Branch and a short bushwhack to the Saddle area.

The trailhead is located on the right side of FS 177-1. There are some large boulders and a small wilderness sign at the trailhead. The trail begins with a gradual descent. After about 0.25 miles, there is a small trail on the right. This trail leads across a small saddle to a high region in the middle of the Shawvers Run Wilderness Area (See Saddle Trail description).

There are thickets of small hardwoods throughout this region. Approximately 0.75 miles after beginning the hike, there is a small spring on the left. This is the first of three small creeks the trail crosses. After crossing the third creek there is a small clearing. This clearing would be a excellent place for some "off the beaten path" camping.

Once past the clearing the trees become much taller with many large poplar, oak, and hickory all the way to Valley Branch. The trail bends to the right and the descent becomes steep. This bend is approximately 1.5 miles from the trailhead. The road then appears to end; however, there is a left turn and the road changes to a footpath which drops sharply before resuming a more moderate slope.

In this area, red blazes marking the FS boundary are visible. There are also small wilderness signs along the boundary. At the end of the trail is a clearing and shack belonging to an organization called the Pond Hunting Club. The hunting camp is reached at 2.2 miles.

A short hike downhill, 0.4 miles, is the Valley Branch Area. The hike is actually a bushwhack. Follow the small creek which flows next to the hunting club down to the Valley Branch. This area is very beautiful and is worth the effort to see.

Valley Branch Trail/Bushwhack   6

Length: 1.5 Miles
Time: 2.0 Hours
Elevation Change: 1,000 Feet
Difficulty: Moderately
USGS Map: Potts Creek
Trailhead: Valley Branch Access Trail

How To Get There

Via the Valley Branch Acces trail.

Trail Description

There are several areas in the Valley Branch section of the Shawvers Run Wilderness which are very beautiful. Most notably is where the Valley Branch drops through a very narrow ravine. This area of large hemlocks, white pines, and cove hardwoods is splendid. There are also large thickets of rhododendron located throughout the area. The distance of the drop is short, less than a 0.5 miles, but the scenery is great.

There is a small trail which leads up the Valley Branch, following what appears to be an old wagon road. This wagon road leads up the creek to a small clearing. There is a deer stand in this clearing. At the clearing, the trail crosses the creek and becomes much harder to follow as mountain laurel crowds the trail. However, after clearing the brush the trail is again easily visible and continues to climb toward the saddle. This road finally ends about 0.5 miles from the top of the saddle. This short bushwhack, which is not overly difficult, leads to the Saddle Trail (See Saddle Trail description).

There is also a road which heads to the south from the area where the Valley Branch enters the narrow defile. This road leads out of the wilderness area and into a clearing in the Hanging Rock Valley. This road eventually leads to private property.

Thunder Ridge Wilderness

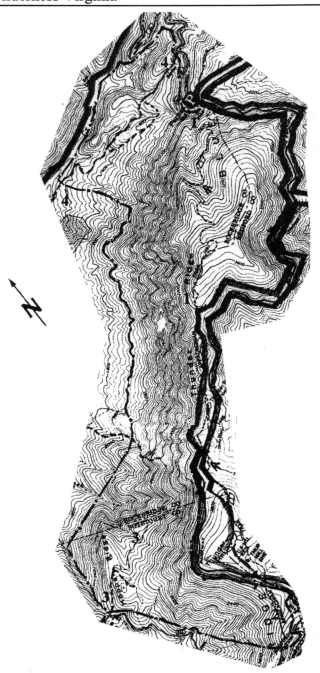

Thunder Ridge

Thunder Ridge is a small wilderness located in Rockbridge and Botetourt Counties about seventeen miles south of Lexington, Virginia. This wilderness area is situated in the Glenwood Ranger District of the Jefferson National Forest. Thunder Ridge occupies an area of 2,450 acres and was declared a wilderness by Congress in 1984.

The wilderness is located on the western slope of the Blue Ridge near Apple Orchard Mountain. It is located on a steep slope called Thunder Ridge. The Blue Ridge Parkway forms most of the eastern boundary, while Forest Service road 35 forms the northern boundary. The region is rugged and unforgiving. The ridge climbs rapidly from the western boundary on the slope of Thunder Ridge to the crest of the mountain. In some areas the angle of the slope is close to seventy degrees. The area near the top is very dry. However, farther down the ridge, in some cases almost on the western boundary, there are small springs which feed both the East Fork and Elk Creek. Elevations range from 1,320 feet to almost 4,225 feet near the top of Apple Orchard Mountain.

There are only a few trails in the wilderness, due to the rugged nature of the land. The major trail lies across the top of the ridge. The Appalachian Trail travels through Thunder Ridge in two places for a combined total of approximately 4.3 miles. The only other maintain trail is a horse trail located near Forest Service road 35. One other area to hike is near the Hopper Ridge which is located at the southern end of the wilderness. Hopper Ridge is difficult to hike in the summer. All total, there is about eight miles of trail to hike.

The forest in this wilderness cover a range of species. Cove species such as tulip poplar, oak, and hemlock inhabit many of the sheltered regions of the wilderness. Some of these trees are very large. Near the crest of Apple Orchard Mountain there is an interesting mix of species, not only are the hardwoods such as red and white oak present, but common persimmon is also represented in large quanities. Due to the high elevation, small red spruce and yellow birch can also be found. The dry western slopes with their harsh environment support species such as pitch pine, Virginia pine, and chestnut oak. There are many flowers found in this wilderness area; wild columbine, pink lady's slipper, trillium, purple flowering raspberry, and fire pink are examples of a few. Mountain laurel and rhododendron are also found in great quantities.

The Appalachian Trail is the only trail which is used heavily.

The rest of the wilderness has few visitors. If seeking solitude the lower half of the wilderness is the place to find it. One note of caution regarding the lower half of the wilderness area: The land fronting the wilderness has been heavily logged making access difficult. However, there are ways in. Finally, it appears that this area might see a significant number of hunters during hunting season. Be advised that it is best not to hike here during hunting season. However, if hiking is done, remember to wear blaze orange.

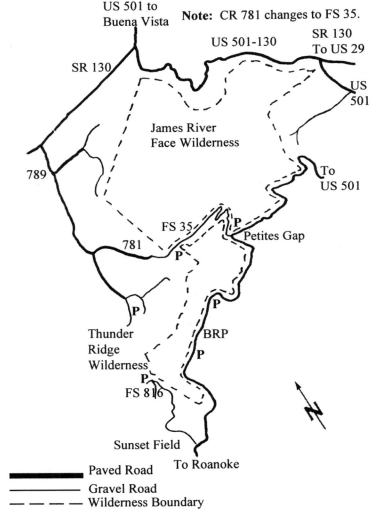

Appalachian Trail 1

Length: 3.3 Miles
Time: 2.0 Hours
Difficulty: Moderate/Difficult
Elevation Change: 1,300 Feet
USGS Maps: Arnold Valley
Trailhead: BRP and FS 35

How To Get There

For the southern parking area, take the BRP to the Thunder Ridge Overlook Parking Area. The parking area is between mileposts 74 and 75. The northern parking area is located on FS 35 about 0.1 miles from the intersection of FS 35 and the BRP. The intersection is near milepost 71. This is the Petites Gap area.

Trail Description

This trail begins near the summit of Thunder Ridge and slowly winds down the ridge to Petites Gap and FS 35. The trail travels through a forest of mixed hardwoods with occasional groves of rhododendron. There are only a few places along the trail for water; therefore, remember to pack enough for the trip. Especially if climbing from Petites Gap to the overlook. This desciption begins at the Thunder Ridge Overlook. The trail is well maintained and well marked with the white blazes of the AT.

The trail begins at the northern end of the parking area. There is a sign for the AT. The first stop on the AT is a manmade rock overlook. The view from the overlook is great. There is an excellent view of Arnold Valley, the Devils Marbles Yard and House Mountain. After leaving the overlook, the trail has a short moderate descent and then it crosses an old road. Near the road crossing, the trail levels out. To the right is a barrier and on the left is a small clearing with a large snag. Just beyond this clearing, the trail climbs again.

After hiking for approximately 0.5 miles, the trails crosses the boundary of the Thunder Ridge Wilderness and begins to descend. There is a huge oak which fell some time ago and the trail wraps around the tree. There are many trees with very black fissured bark indicative of common persimmon. There are also many striped maples. Striped maple is an interesting tree in that it has the ability to change its sex throughout its life. The tops of many of the trees are broken and there is a great deal of dead lying on the ground - a sign of several hard winters on the ridge.

At approximately 1.0 miles, the trail begins a long gradual climb. After a bend to the left, there is a small rocky outcrop with a view of Arnold Valley and Devils Marble Yard. Near the summit of this small ridge, is a camping area with a fire circle. Throughout the area there are many broken trees which give the trail a surreal look. After 1.5 miles, the trail bends to the right and begins to descend. There are many rocky places and the rocks are loose, so be careful of the ankles.

The trail bends to the left and there is a small flat area on the downhill side. This is an excellent place to camp, as there is a rock firepit and a small spring. A short trail leads into this camping area. A large basswood tree is located near the center of the small clearing and should provide excellent shade. There is also a sign about the water quality. The water has not been tested and proper precautions should be utilized before drinking it.

Just beyond the campsite the trail becomes steeper. Logs have been placed on the trail to prevent erosion. About midway down this steep section there is a old road which exits to the left. After a left switchback, the trail begins to level out and the grade is more moderate. There is also a view of Highcock Knob, in the James River Face Wilderness, just past the switchback.

About 2.5 miles into the hike, the trail crosses a small, rocky creek. There is water here but again, it should be treated. The trail enters a thicket of rhododendron and mountain laurel, with hemlock and white pine dominating the overstory. The area is cool and shady. The trail forks here and the AT climbs up to the right. The left fork reconnects with the AT a little farther down the trail. The trail bends to the right and climbs over the shoulder of the mountain. The grade of the trail is now easy.

When the trail tops the shoulder, it begins a final descent to FS 35. There is a switchback to the right and then a switchback to the left. The forest in this area is old growth with some very impressive trees. There is another switchback to the right and just beyond the switchback is a Thunder Ridge Wilderness sign. Near the junction with FS 35 is a sign with distances of 4.6 miles to the Thunder Ridge Trail Shelter and 7 miles to FS 812.

The AT passing through a rhododendron thicket on Thunder Ridge.

AT Near the FAA Installation 2

Length: 0.8 Miles
Time: 45 Minutes
Difficulty: Easy
Elevation Change: 325 Feet
USGS Maps: Arnolds Valley
Trailhead: Near milepost 76 on the BRP

How To Get There

The parking area is on the east side of the road near milepost 76. There is a small road and a gate. Remember not to block the gate. To reach the trailhead hike south on the BRP about 100 yards

Trail Description

This section of the AT is very short and clearly marked by white blazes. The trail, which is well maintain, is an easy ascent to the summit of Apple Orchard Mountain. The summit is a clear grassy area but the scenery is marred by an FAA installation.

The trail exits the Parkway to the south and enters the wilderness area just a short distance from the parking area. The area is flat and the trail meanders lazily through the woods. Red oak and maple form the overstory, while the understory is composed of small chestnut, mountain laurel, and striped maple. Just before a small clearing, the trail exits the wilderness and re-enters the wilderness south of the clearing. In the clearing and along its edges, there are many small red spruce and yellow birch, trees indicative of elevations over 4,000 feet.

Once back into the primitive area, the trail climbs at a moderate rate. The forest is composed of mixed hardwoods with gnarled chestnut oak the dominant species. The trail continues to climb to an area of boulders. Here there is one large boulder that is held up by two others forming a small tunnel. The trail passes through this tunnel. This tunnel is 0.5 miles from the trailhead. After the tunnel there is a series of stone steps and the trail is very steep. When the trail makes a switchback to the left, the grade begins to moderate somewhat. This switchback is followed by a switchback to the right. The trail exits the woods and enters a large clearing at the top of Thunder Ridge.

At the entrance of the clearing is a Thunder Ridge Wilderness sign. In the clearing, turn right and climb into the grassy clearing. There is good view in every direction. The trail travels through the clearing and then begins a long descent to FS 816. At the summit, there is a sign for Apple Orchard Mountain, elevation 4,224 feet. In the middle of the clearing is a small trail to the left that leads to some boulders. These boulders form the summit of Apple Orchard Mountain. There is also an FAA intallation at the summit.

Hopper Ridge   3

Length: 0.9 Miles
Time: 45 Minutes
Difficulty: Easy
Elevation Change: 300 Feet
USGS Maps: Arnold Valley
Trailhead: FS 816

How To Get There

Take the BRP to the Sunset Field parking area near milepost 78. Take FS 816 out of the parking area and travel 3.0 miles. At the gate and the junction with the road to Apple Orchard Falls, there is parking on the right.

Trail Description

This is a short dead end trail on the southern end of Thunder Ridge. The trail is not marked with any blazes but is fairly easy to follow. It follows an old road cut around a shoulder on the western side of the mountain. One note, in the summer this trailhead is impossible to see as the section under the powerlines is choked with weeds. In fact, the best time to hike this trail would be after the first hard frost of the fall season.

The trail begins at the powerlines coming up the mountain. After crossing a small earth barrier, it turns left and begins to climb. There is one yellow blaze near the beginning of the trail, but no other blazes are visible. The grade is moderate and the climb is steady. After a short distance a small road exit to the left. The area is a tangle of muscadine grape vines and windfall; however, the trail is easy to follow and fairly easy to hike. Another fire road exits to the left about 0.3 miles.

After the fire road, the trail flattens out and the hike becomes much easier. There is fork in the trail at the right bend. One branch of the fork continues straight and is less clear, the other bends to the right. The right fork continues its easy grade. About 0.2 miles from the bend, the trail becomes less clear and more indistinct. Although hard to follow, it bends to the left and flattens out. The trail enters a small, sheltered bowl. In this bowl is a great old growth forest with tree stumps which dwarf the large trees now growing. There is a small clearing in this bowl which would be an excellent primitive campsite. However, remember to pack water as there is none along the trail.

Back at the bend, the left fork parallels the right fork. The only difference is that it is lower on the mountainside and is easier to follow. The grade is easy as the old road contours the mountainside with a slight decrease in elevation. There are stinging nettle along this trail so if hiking in the summer wear long pants. Just past two dead logs the trail crosses a small creek. On the right side of the creek, about 0.1 miles, the trail forks again. The straight fork leads to a dead end. The branch to the left leads to a great campsite about 50 yards off the trail. The area is clear of brush and flat, and there is water nearby. In fact, it is probably used as a hunting camp.

Dogwood flowers in full bloom.

Horse Trail On FS 35 4

Length: 2.1 Miles
Time: 1 Hours
Difficulty: Moderate
Elevation Change: 1000 Feet
USGS Maps: Snowden
Trailhead: FS 35

How To Get There

Take I-81 to Exit #180. Take US 11 south 3.5 miles to US 130. Turn left on SR 130 and proceed 3.2 miles to CR 759. Turn right on CR 759, travel 3.2 miles, and turn left on CR 781. Travel 2.1 miles to a parking area on the right. CR 781 turns becomes FS 35 prior to reaching the parking area. The upper parking area is located on FS 35 about 0.6 miles from the intersection of FS 35 and the BRP.

From Lynchburg, take US 29 and turn West on SR 130 and proceed miles to 29 miles. After crossing the mountain, near Glasgow, SR 130 will turn left. Turn left on CR 759 and follow the above directions.

Trail Description

This little used trail on the northern end of the Thunder Ridge Wilderness follows an old road which terminates in the Marble Springs Area of the James River Face Wilderness. The trail is marked with orange blazes and parallels a small creek over half its distance. The trail passes throughout two distinct forest groups: the first is composed primarily of cove hardwoods, hemlock, and white pine; while the second area contains upland hardwoods such as chestnut oak, red oak, and hickory.

The trail begins at a small parking area located on the right side of the FS 35. After crossing a creek, which can be difficult if the water is high, the trail begins to climb at an easy grade. Throughout the area are hemlock, hickory, oak, poplar, and black cherry. This climb takes the trail away from the creek bottom. After a bend to the left, the trail descends back to the creek. The grade at the creek is easy. The trail makes a big bend to the right and leaves the creek behind.

The climbs becomes moderate when the trail makes a bend to the left and a small road exits to the right. This old road is approximately 0.8 miles from the trailhead and reconnects with the main trail about 0.5 miles farther up the trail. It travels through an area of large white pine and tulip poplar.

Just beyond a bend the trail becomes more moderate and the hemlocks are very large. There are several very large hardwoods in the area, also. The road continues straight, but the trail climbs up the side of the creek bank and then rejoins the road after about 200 yards. The purpose of this detour is to allow people on horseback to avoid an old collapsed bridge.

247

There is a left bend and the trail begins a short, steep climb, including a left switchback and then a right switchback. Shortly after these switchbacks, the trail flattens out for a short distance, and the road which exited earlier ties back into the trail. This flat area would be a nice spot for some out of the way camping. This location is approximately 1.3 miles from the trailhead. The trail begins to climb again and the grade continues to be moderate. At 1.5 miles, the trail crosses a small creek, bends to the left, and continues its climb. This region is filled with large hemlock, many of which suffer from blister rust. When the trail climbs out of the creek drainage, the trees become much smaller and copise growth would indicate that logging occured here not too long ago. The trail passes a wilderness sign and then exits on FS 35. However, it continues on the other side of the road in the James River Face Wilderness. It teminates at the AT just above Marble Spring. (See James River Face Wilderness: AT Connector Trail description).

The authors at the summit of Gaudalupe Peak in Texas.

Mark Miller is a teacher, writer, and outdoor enthusiast. He and his wife, Cindy, live in Lexington, Virginia with their three daughters. Mark began hiking in Northern Minnesota at a young age. He has hiked extensively in Montana, North Carolina and Virginia. In addition to hiking, other interests include bicycling and gardening.

Steven Carroll has lived and hiked in Virginia his entire life. Raised in Alleghany County, Steven now resides in Charlottesville where he works for an environmental company. Aside from hiking, Steven enjoys rock climbing, mountain biking, and photography.